Strapped & Harnessed

Hot Girls in Sexy Straps and Leather Lingerie

By **EROTICA PHOTO ART LOVER**

Copyright © Strapped & Harnessed

All rights reserved. No part of this document may be Reproduced or transmitted in any form or by any means, electronic, mechanical, photocopying, Recording, or otherwise, without prior written permission of erotica photo art lover.

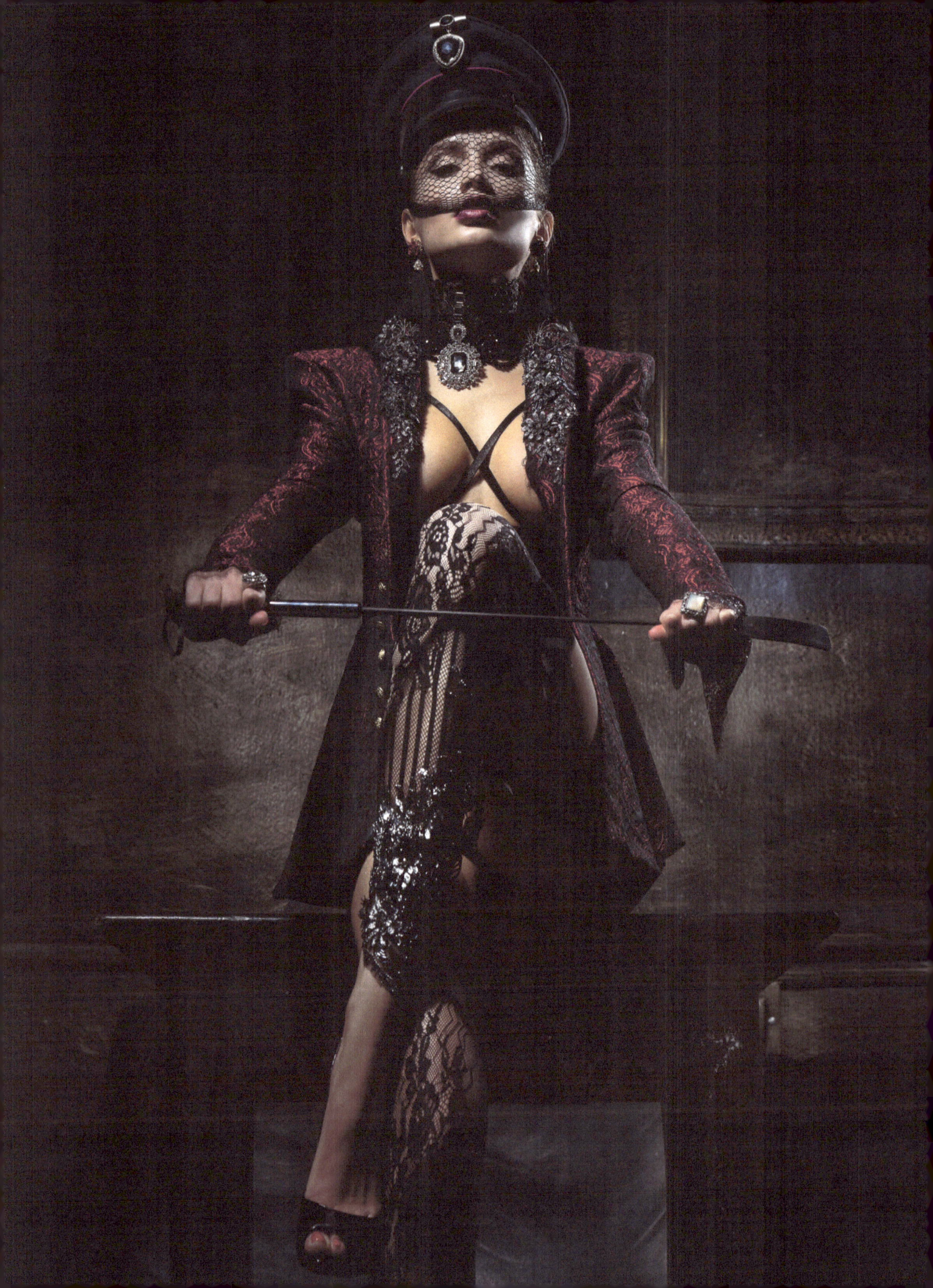

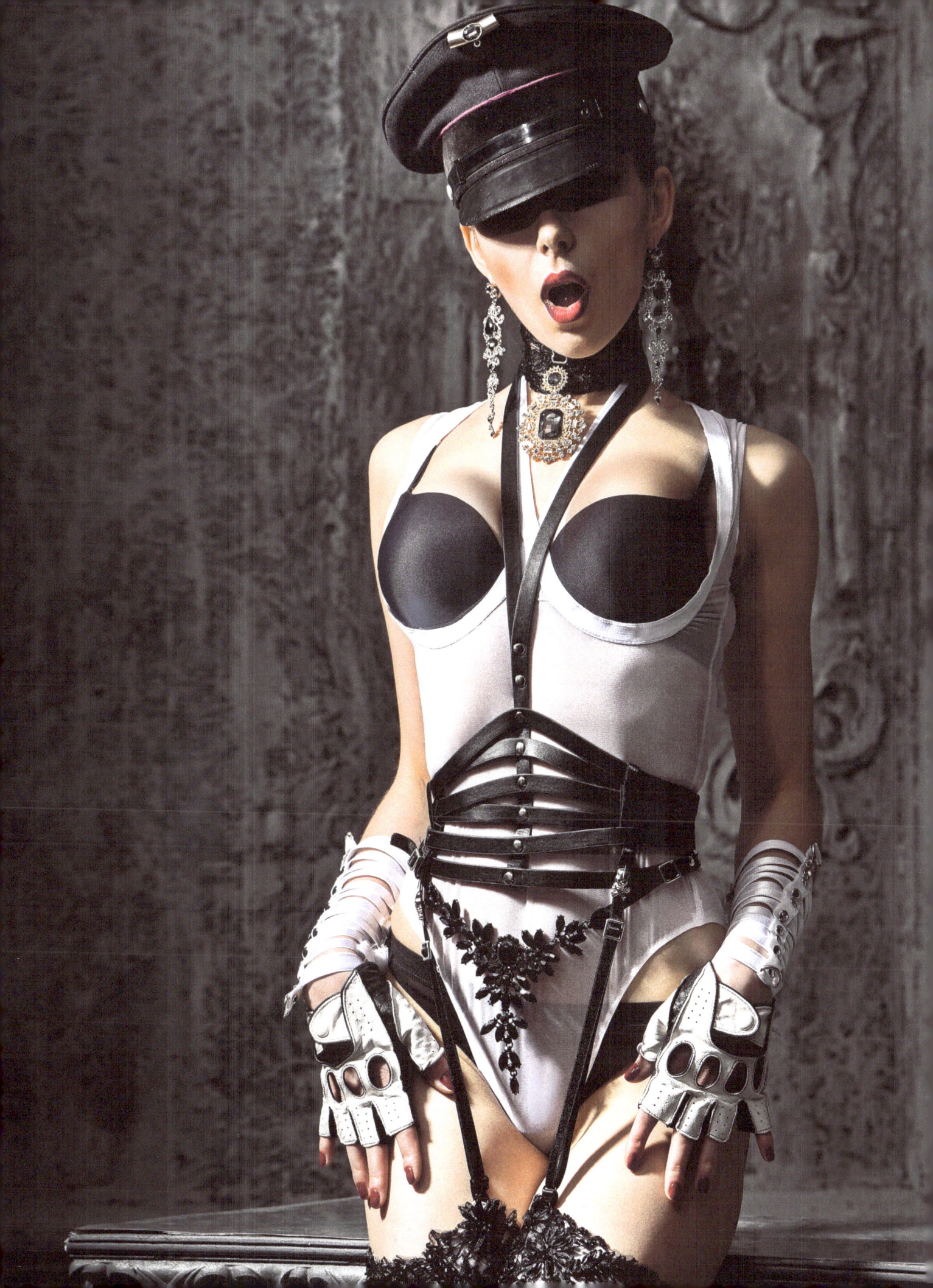

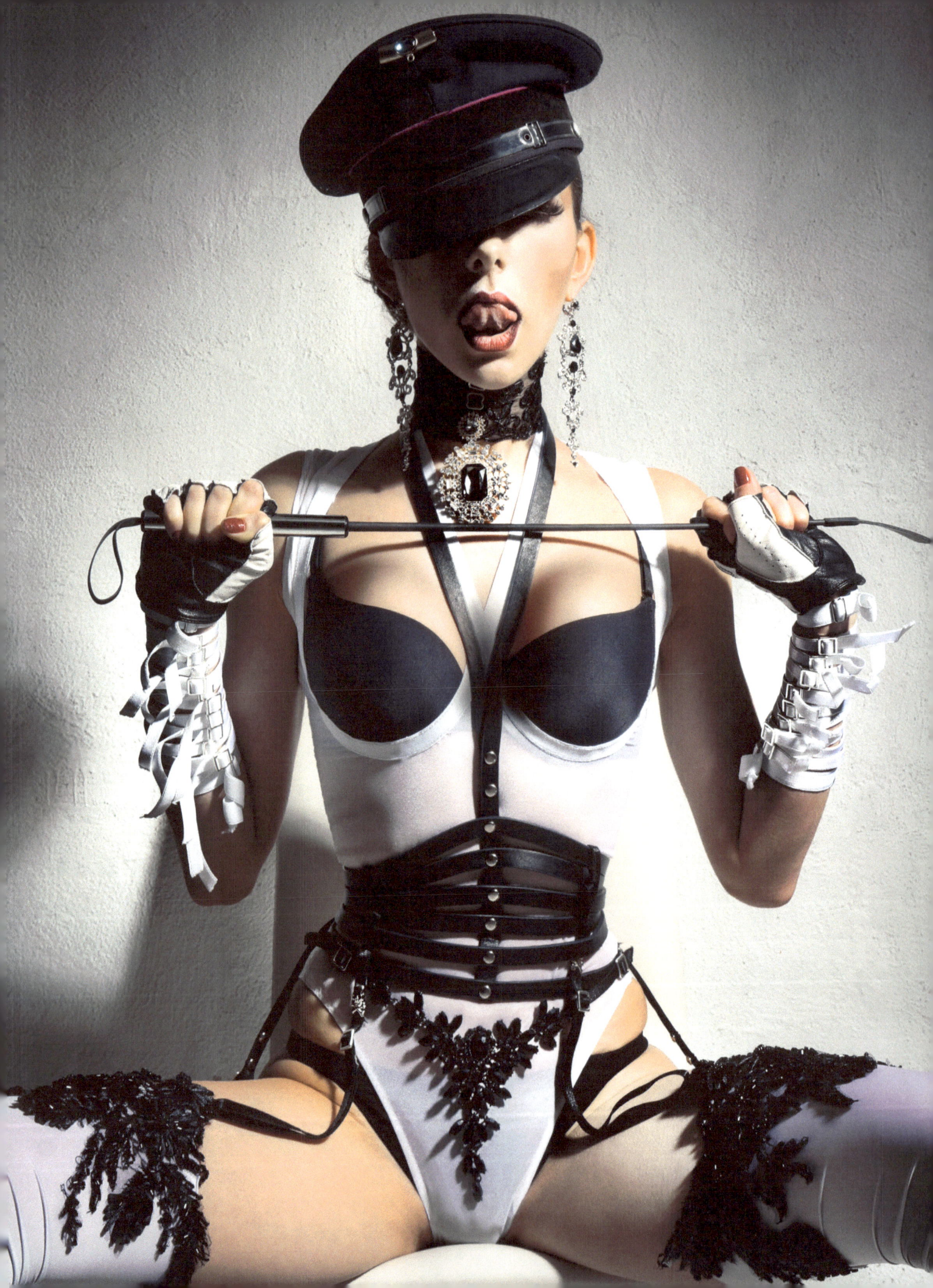

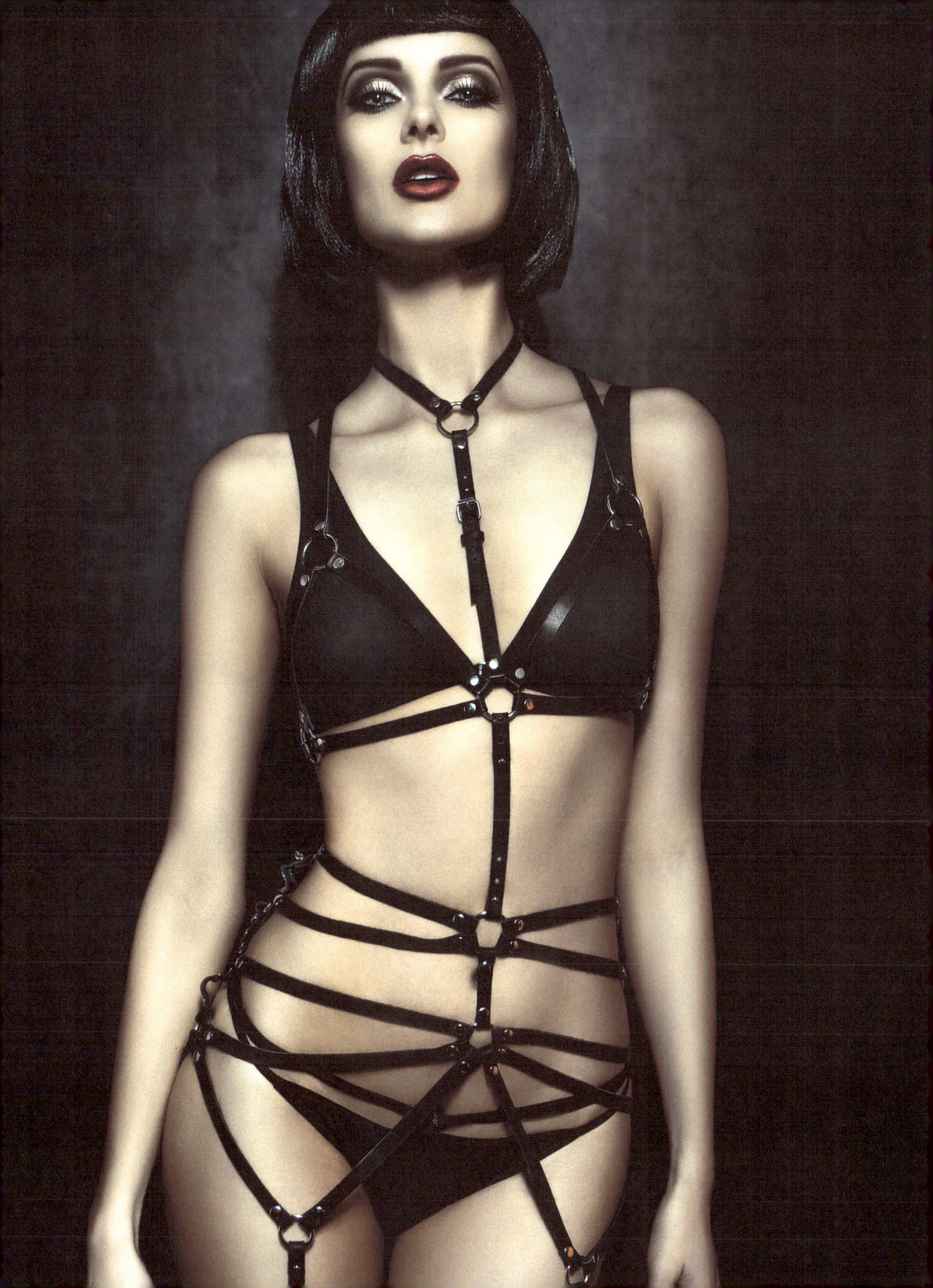

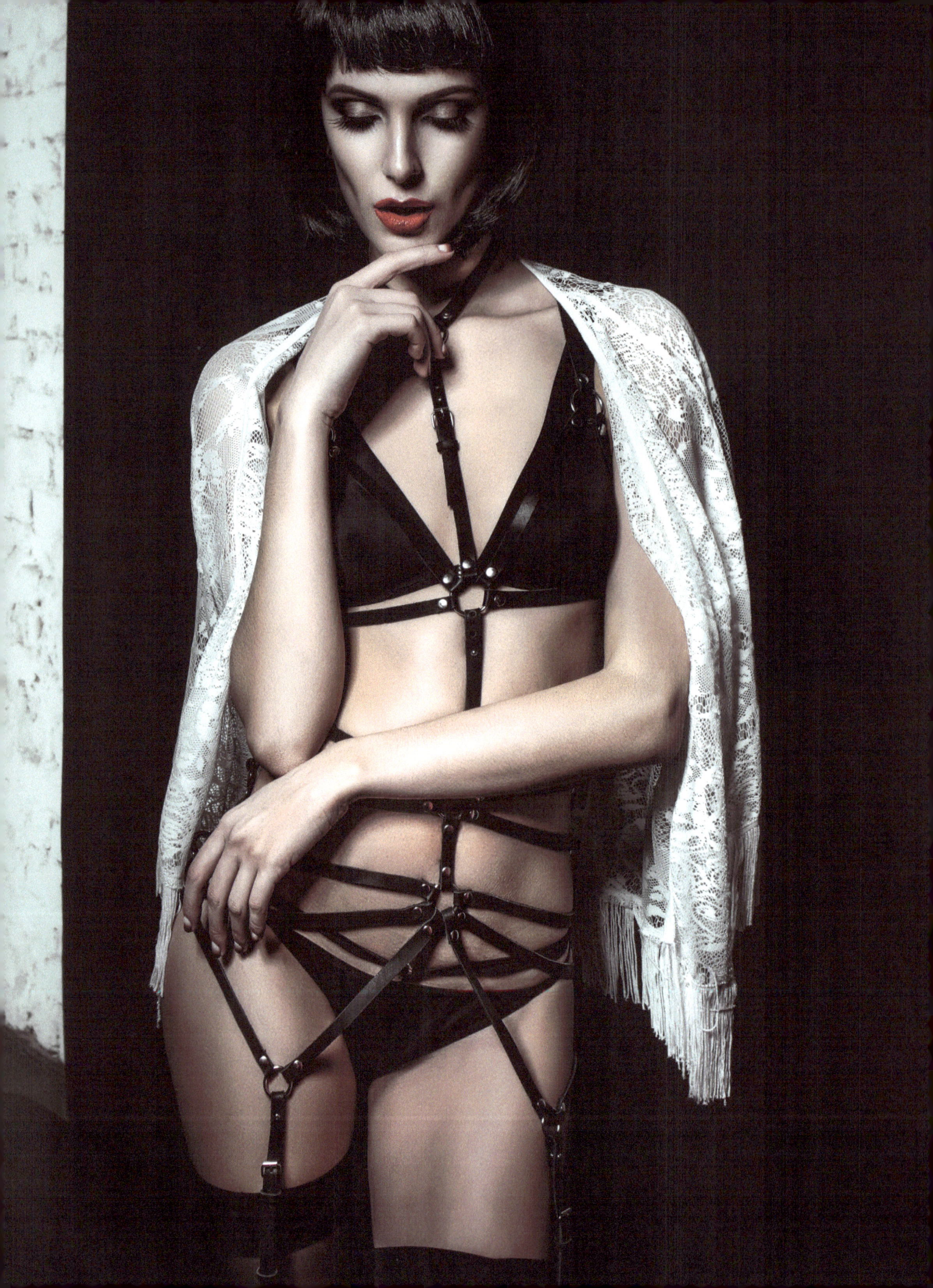

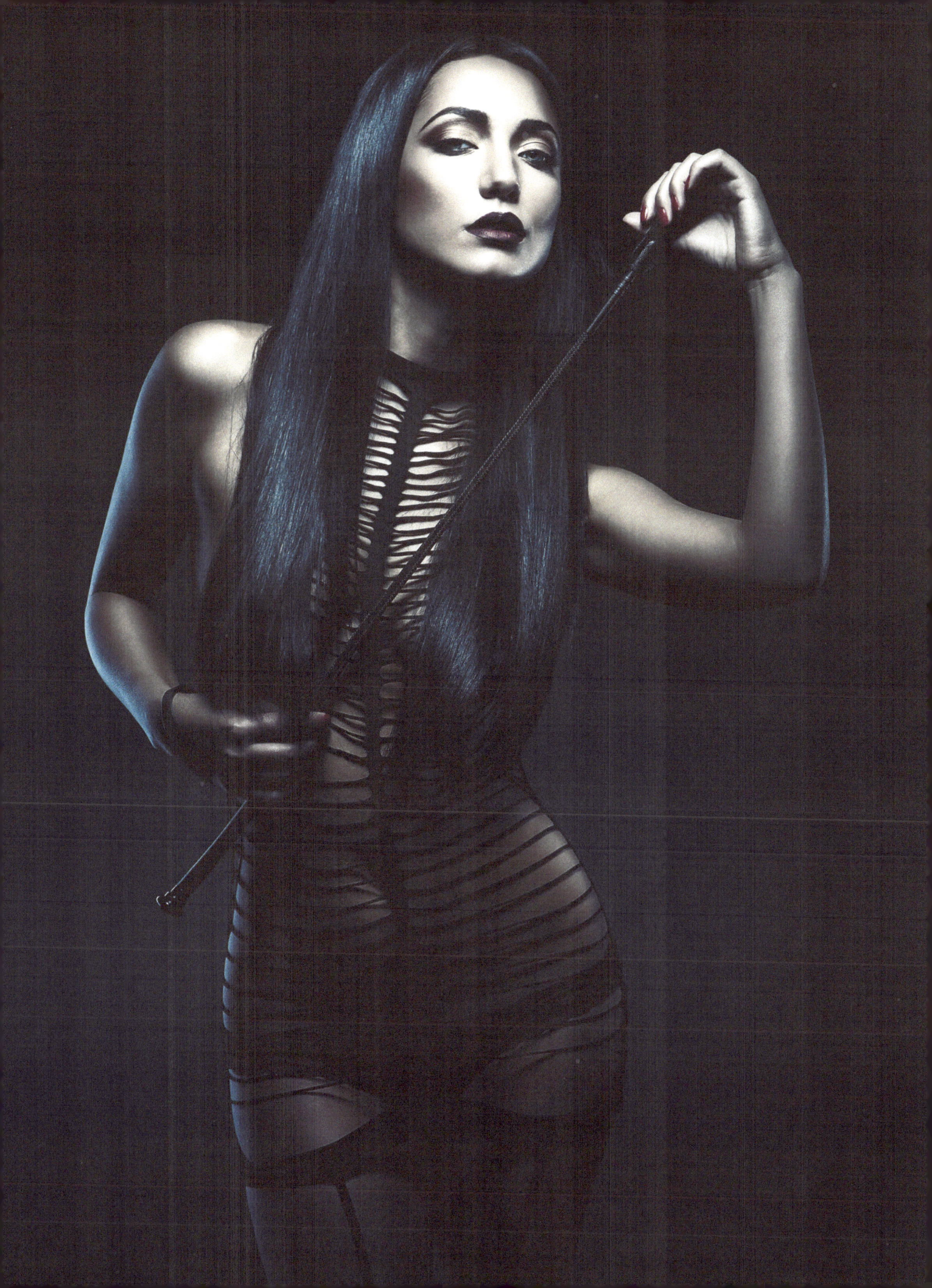

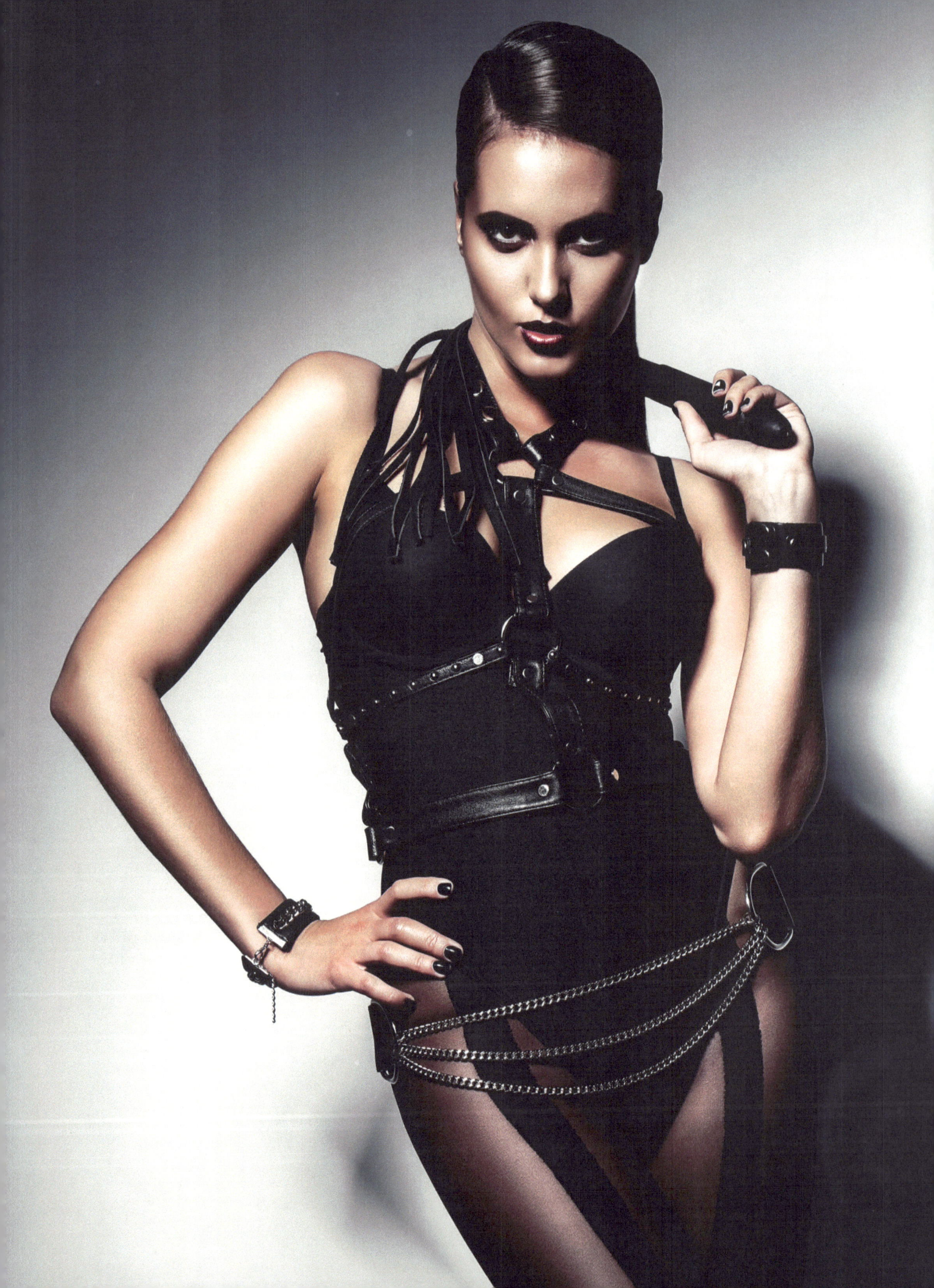

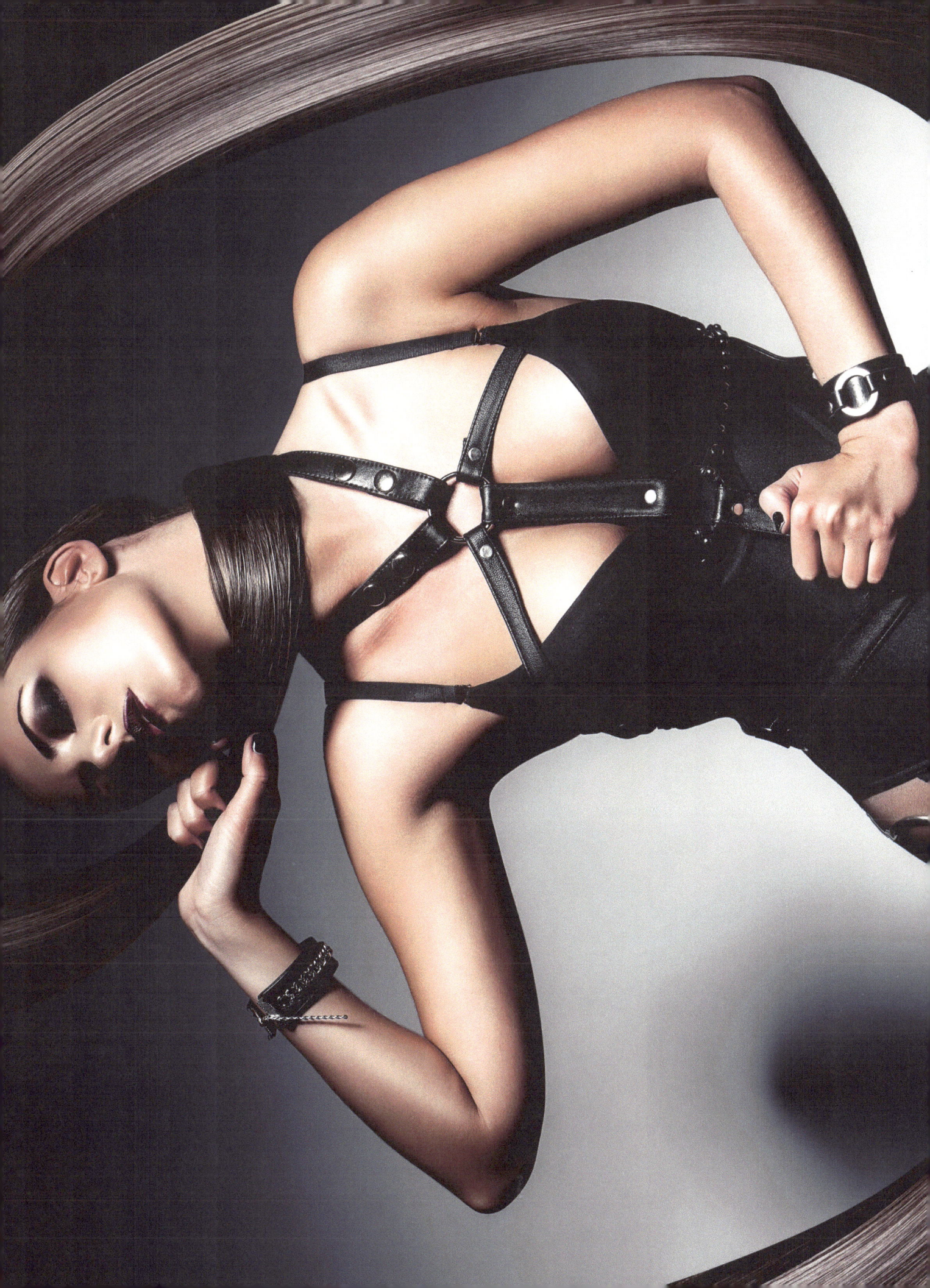

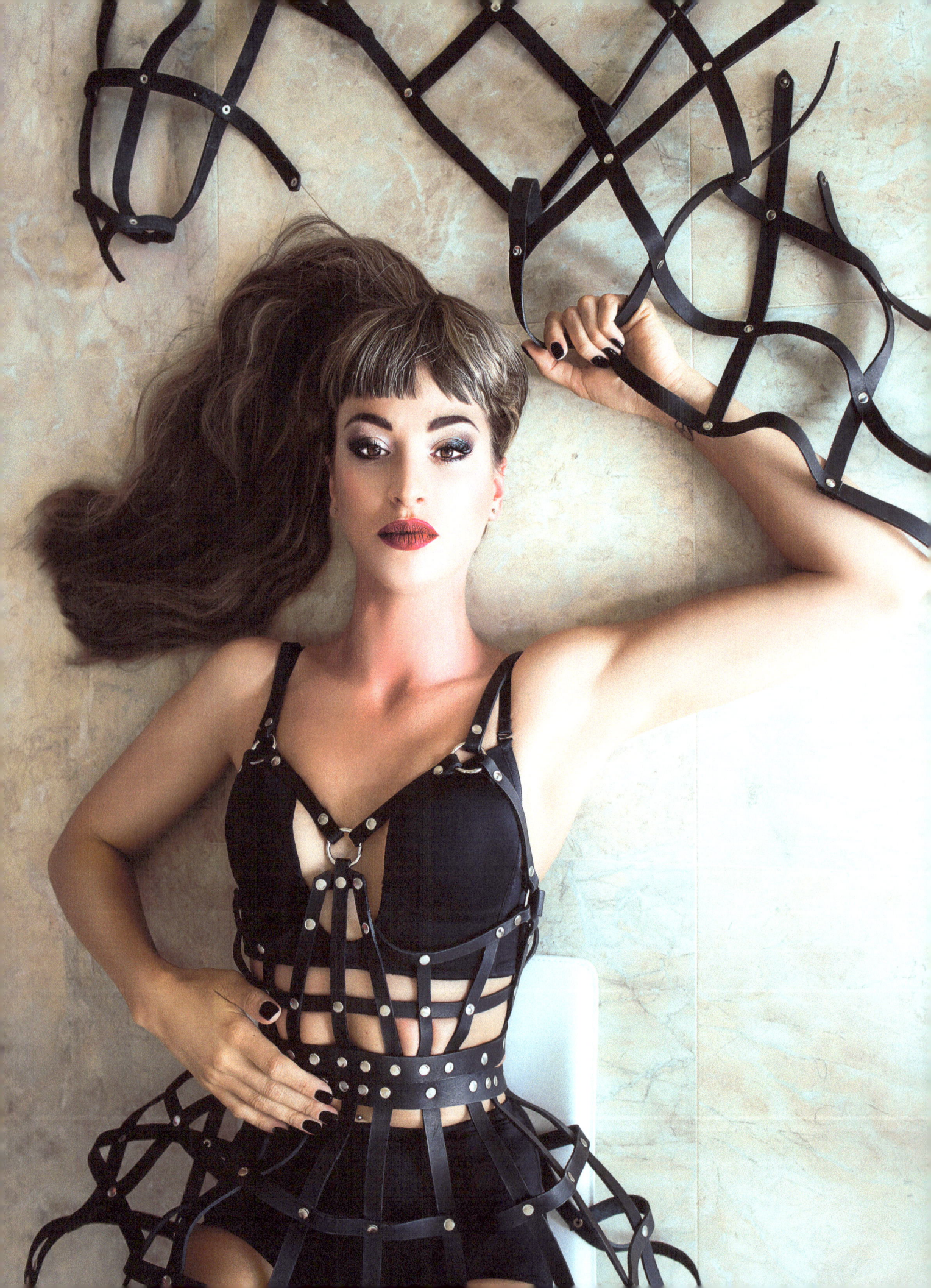

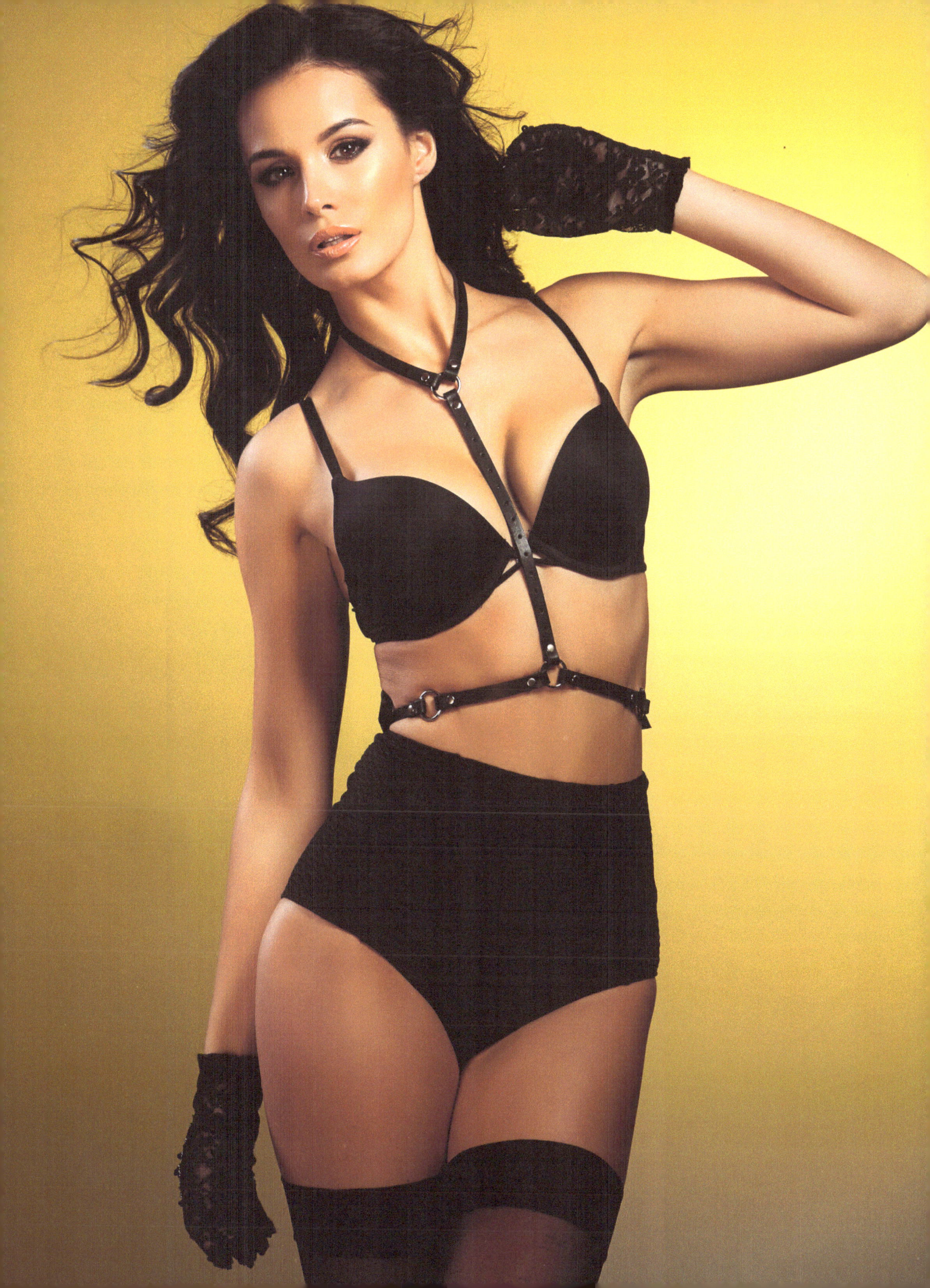

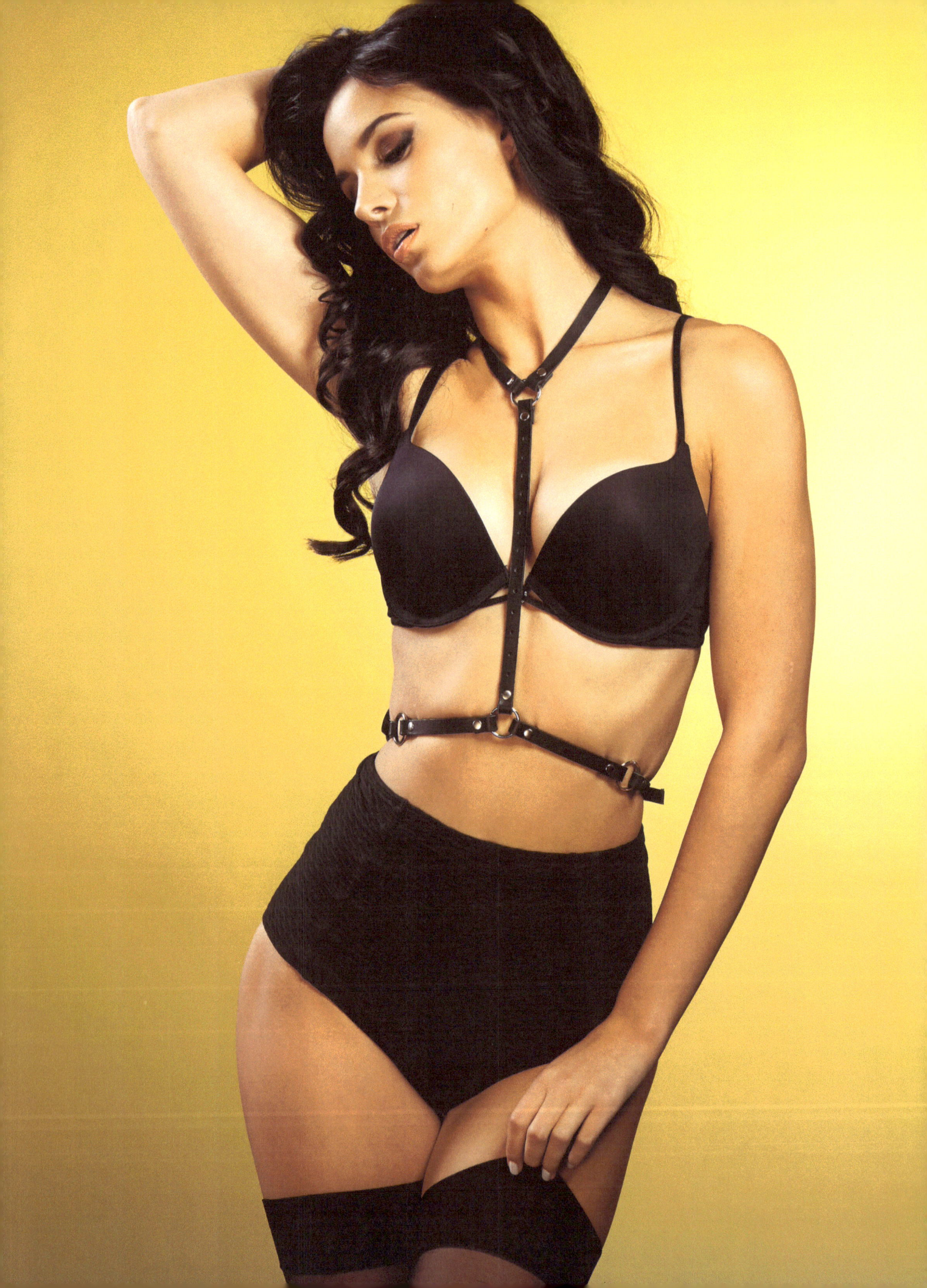

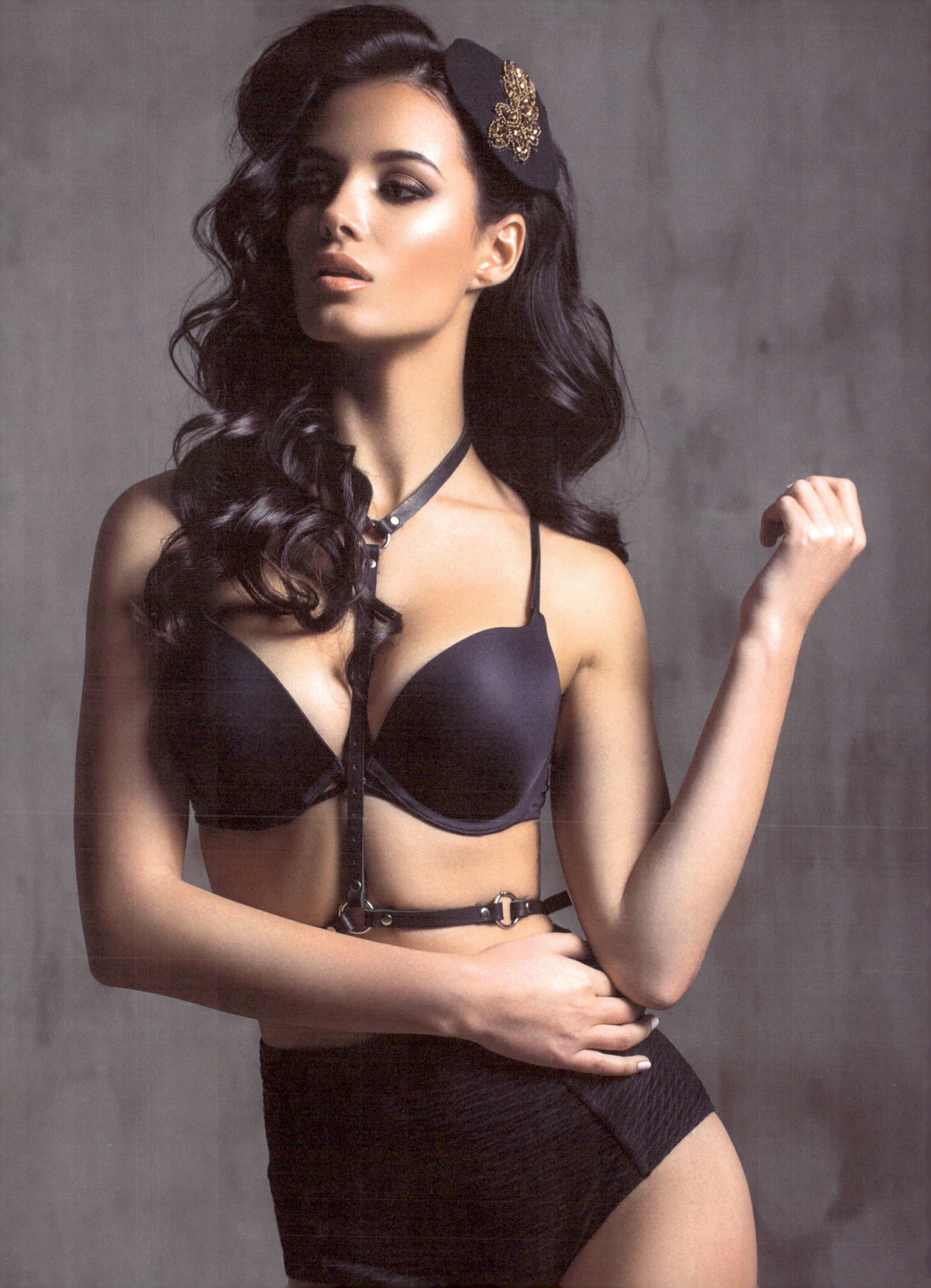

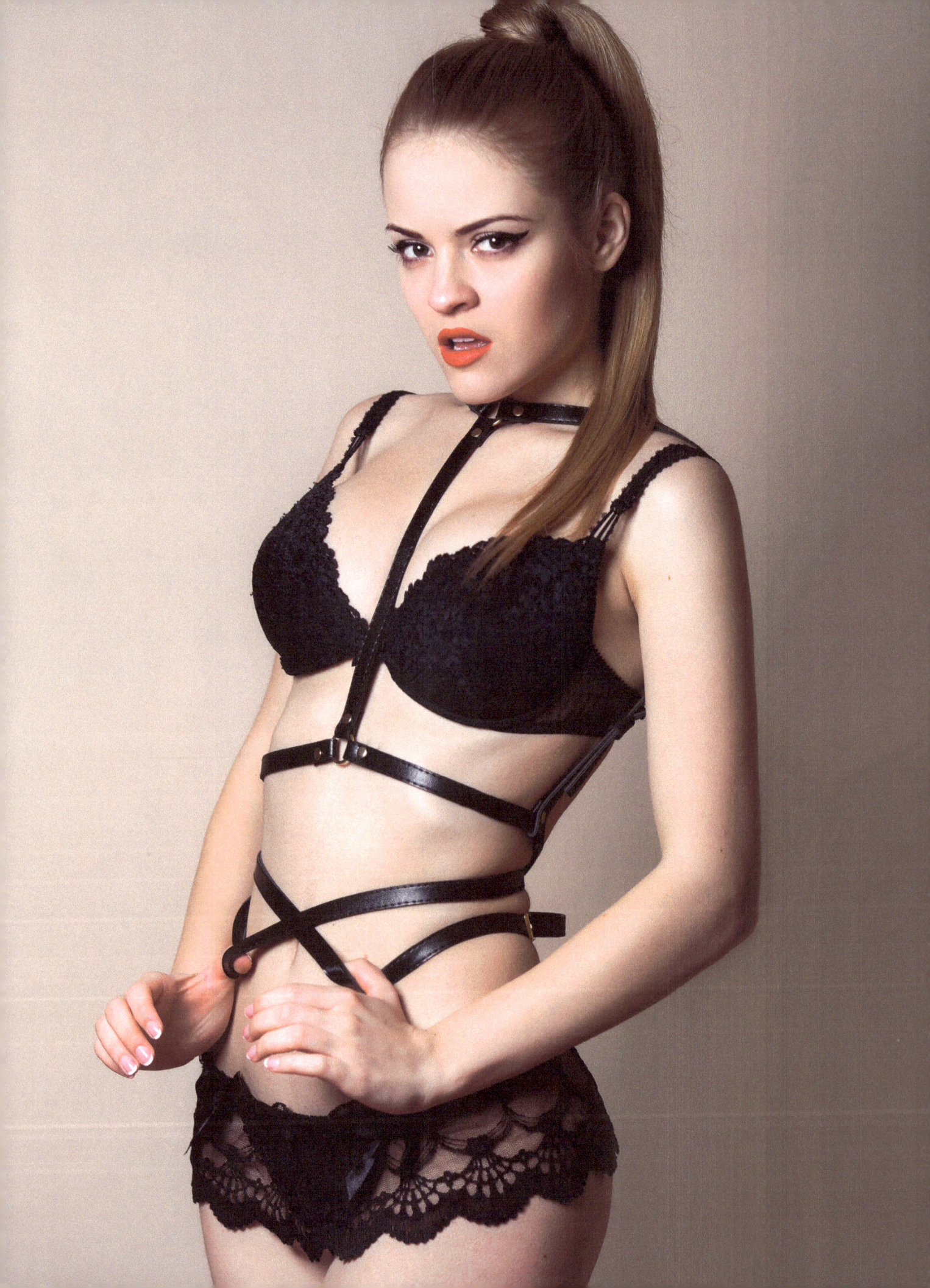

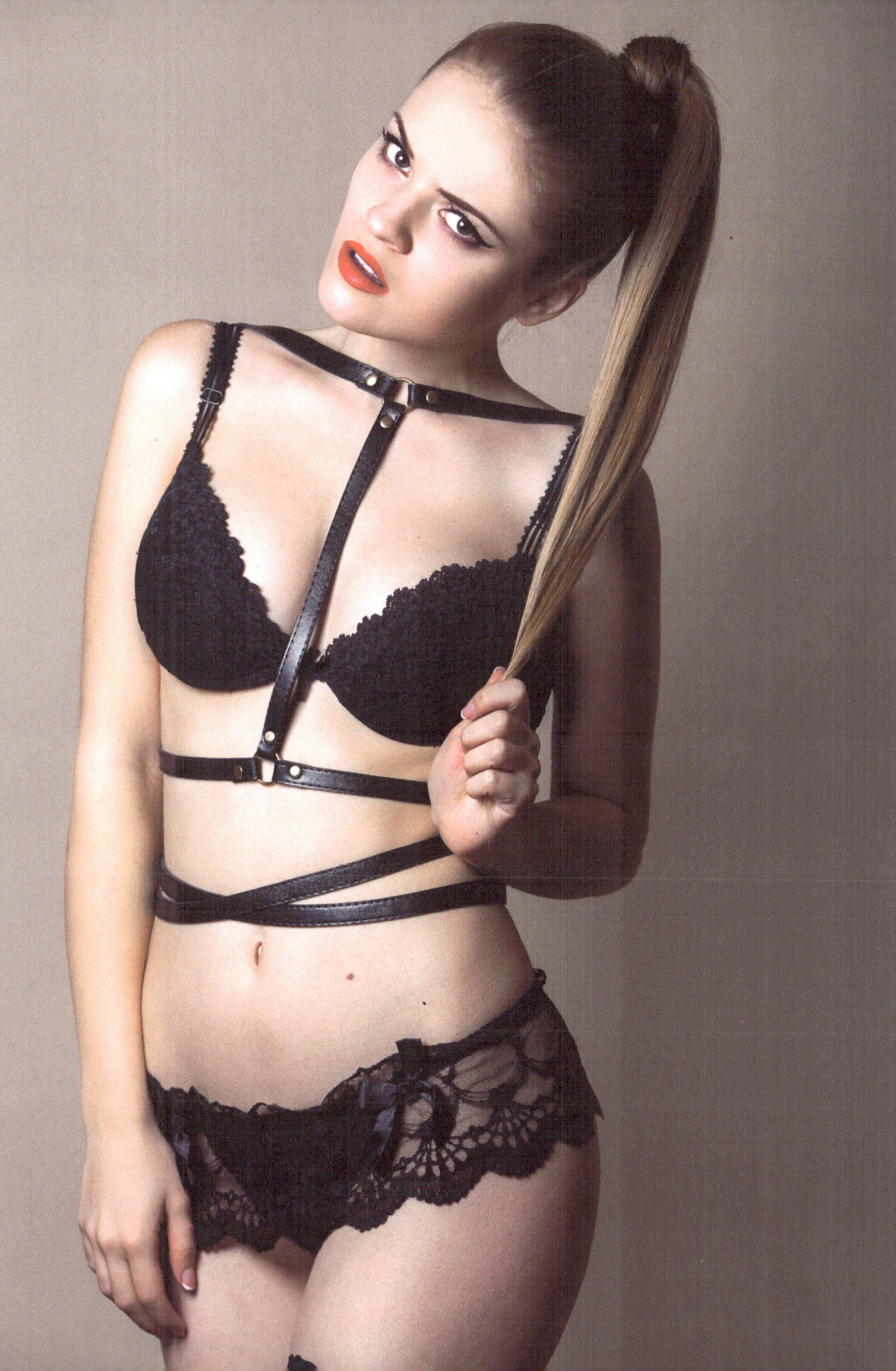

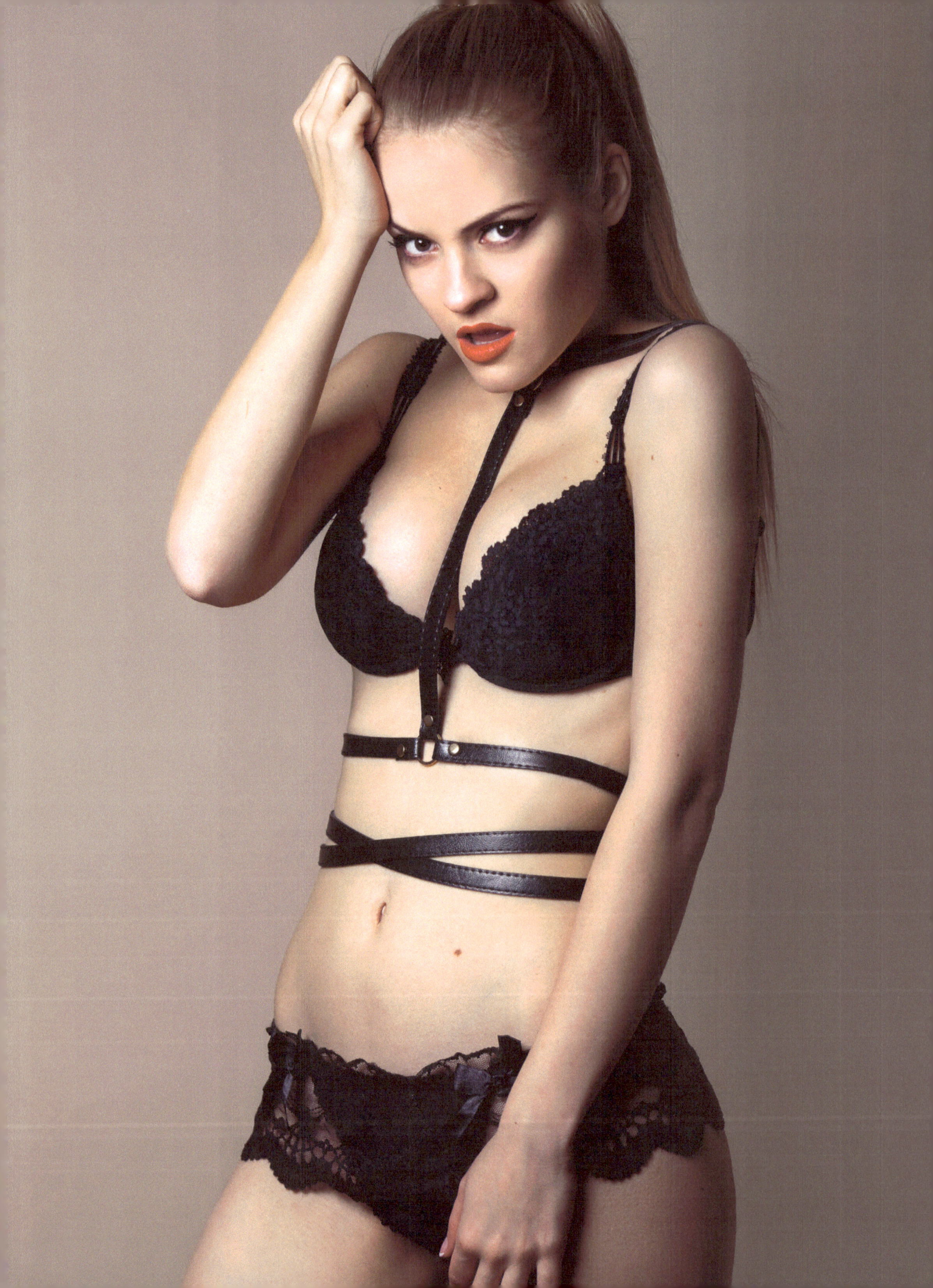

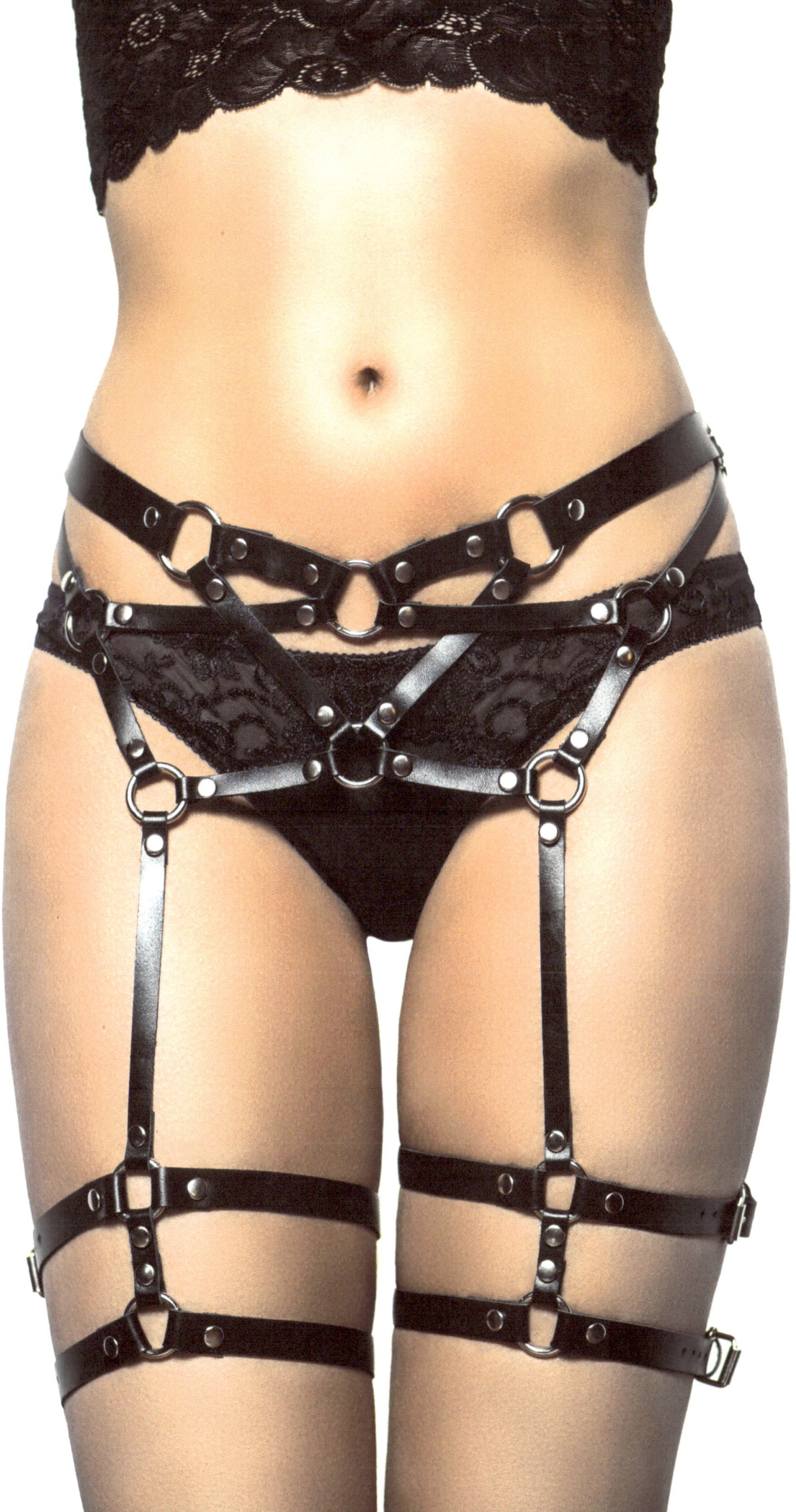

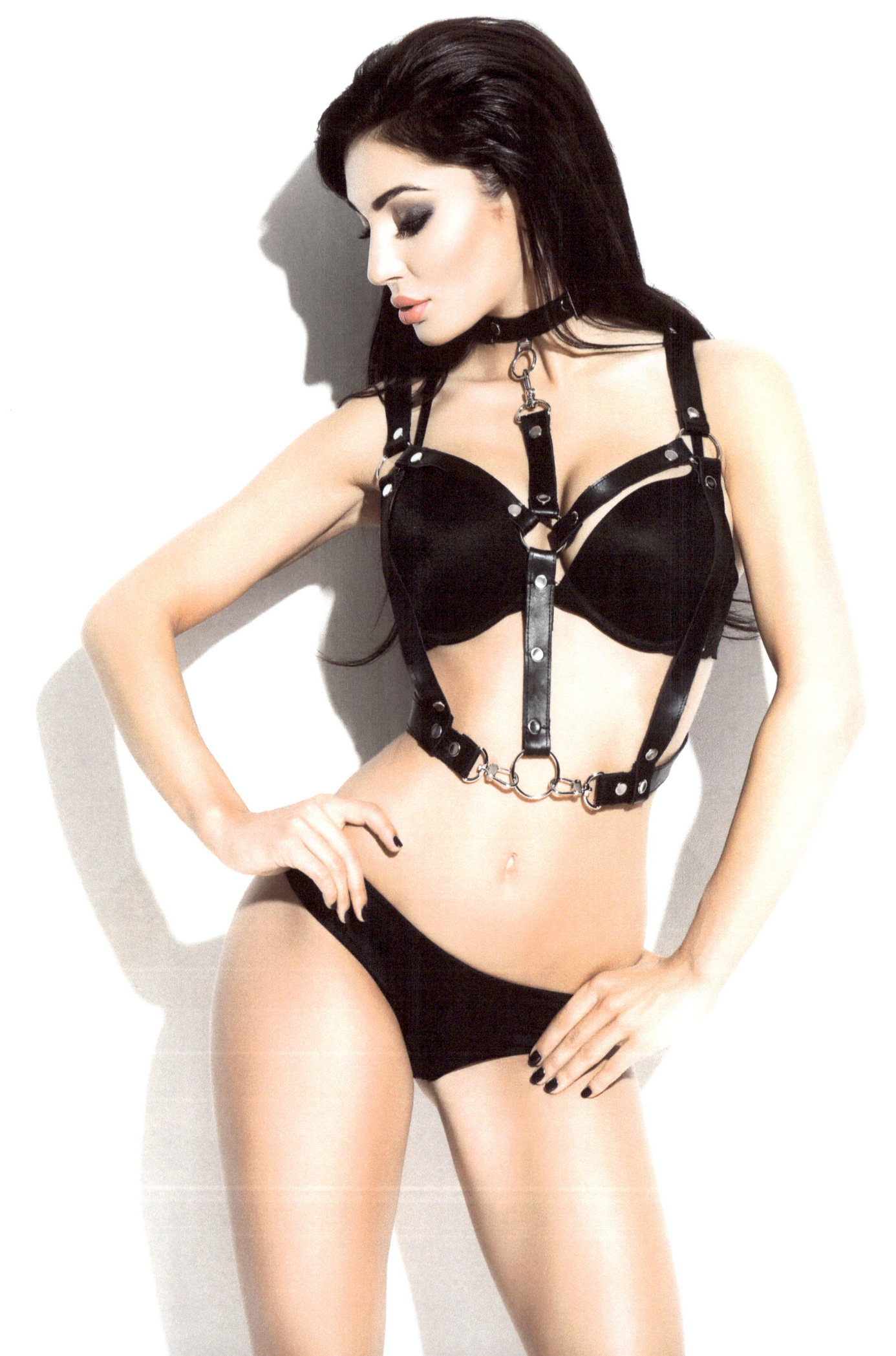

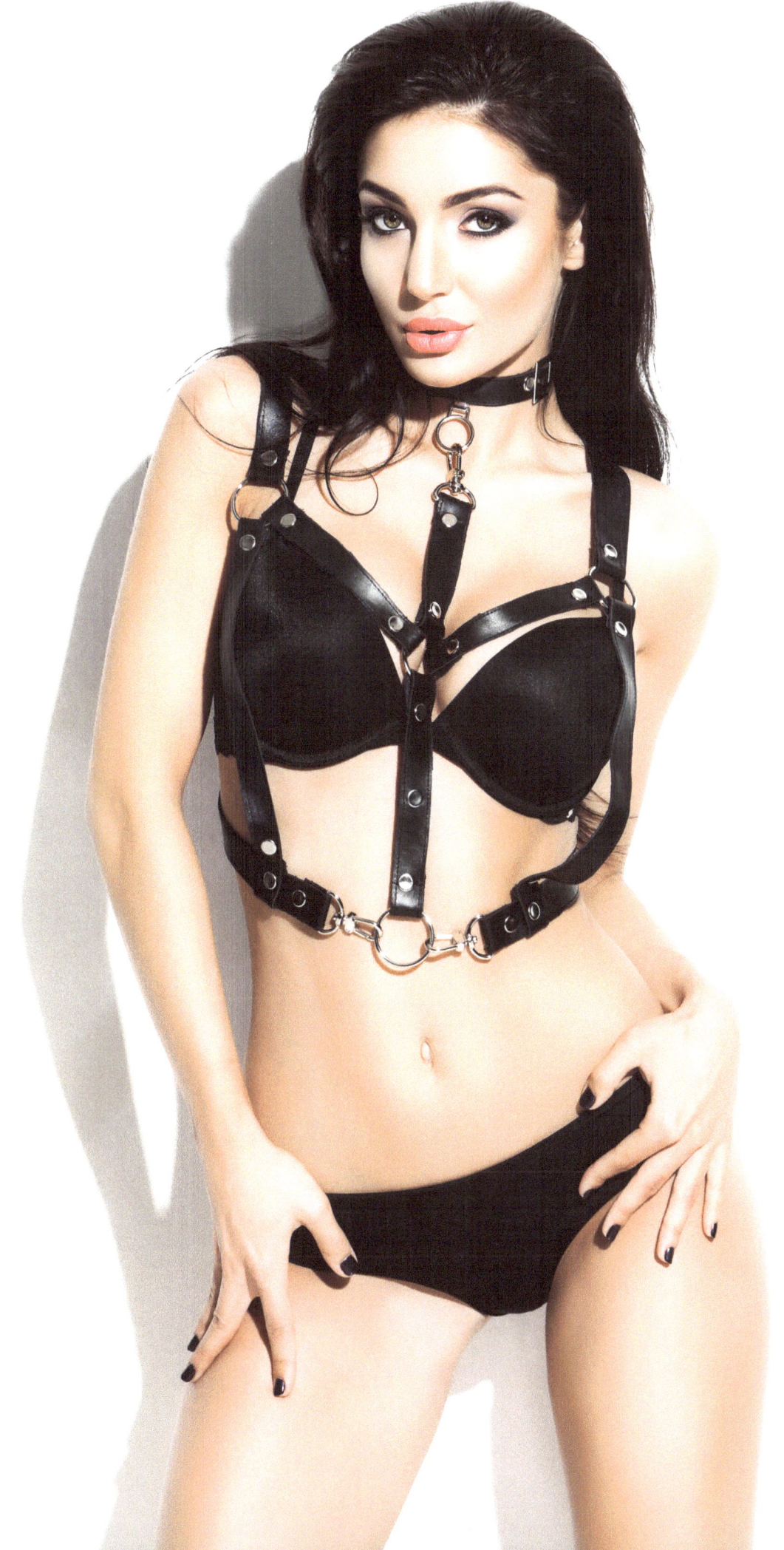

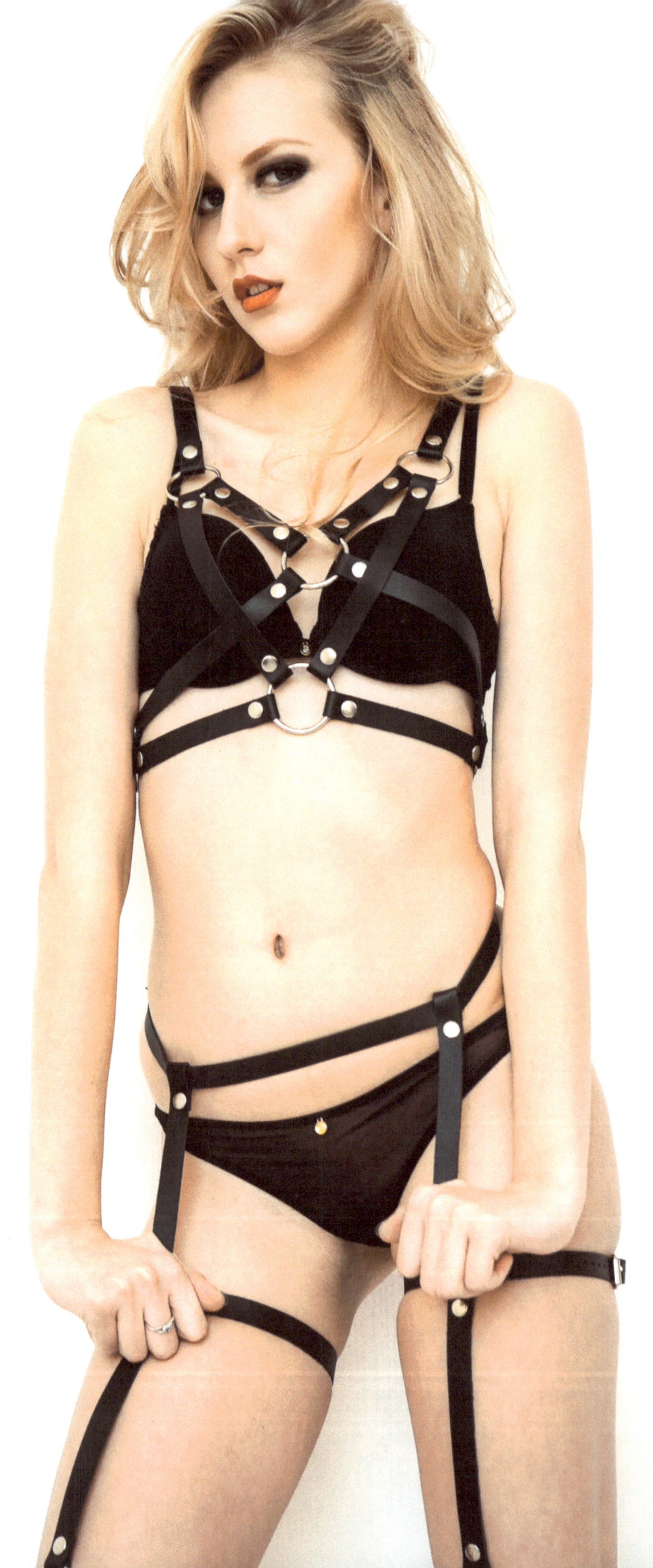

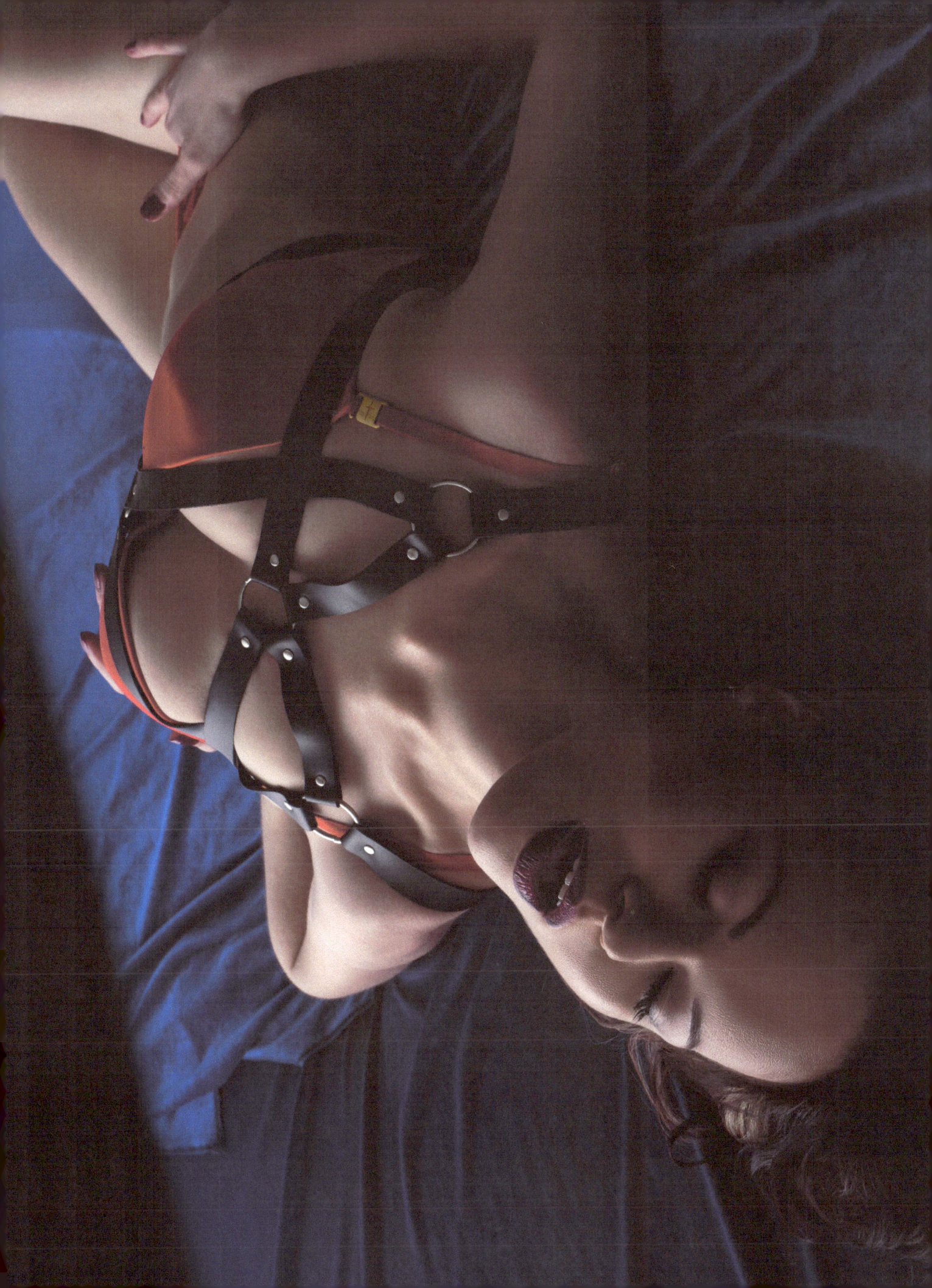

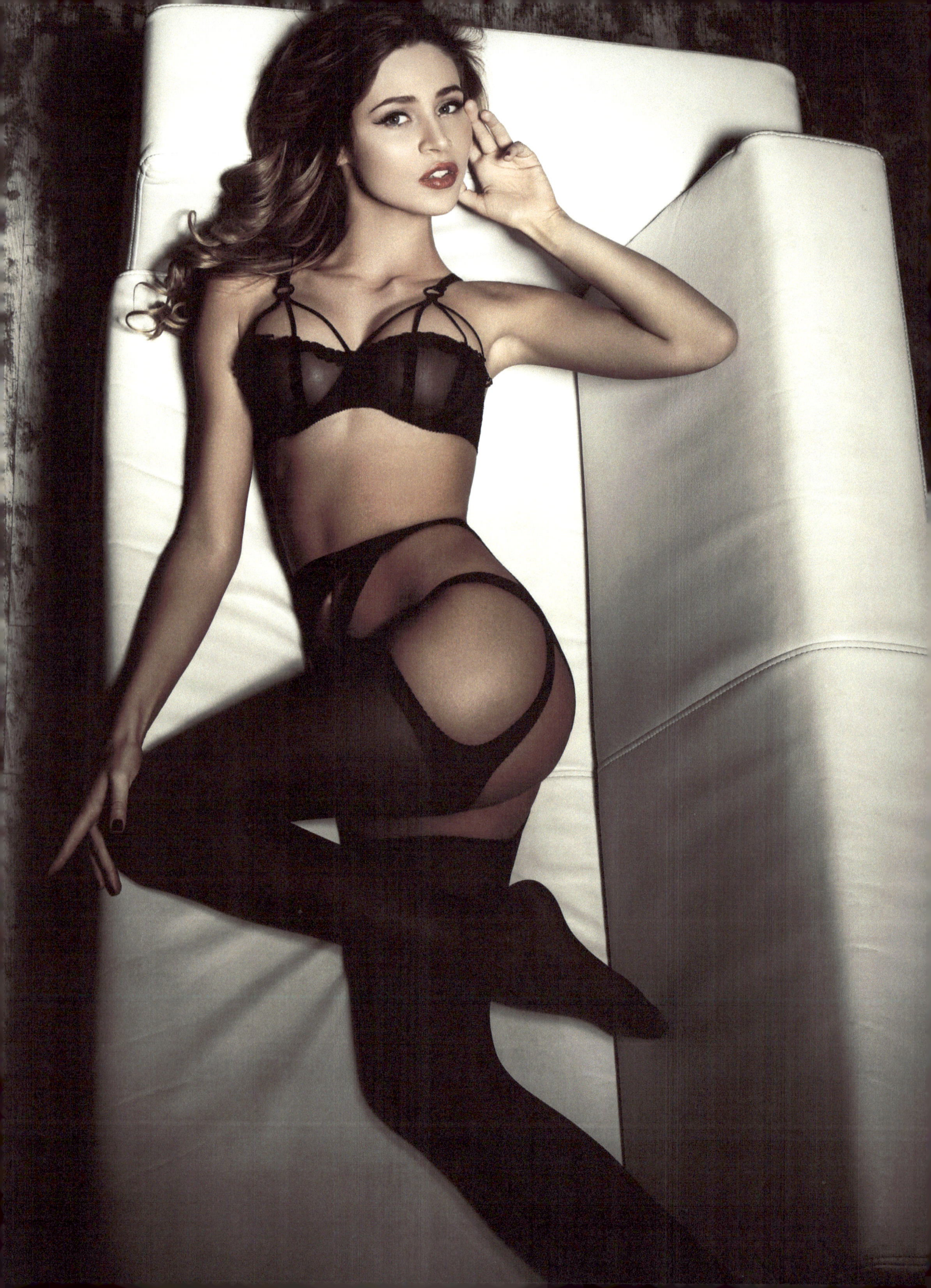

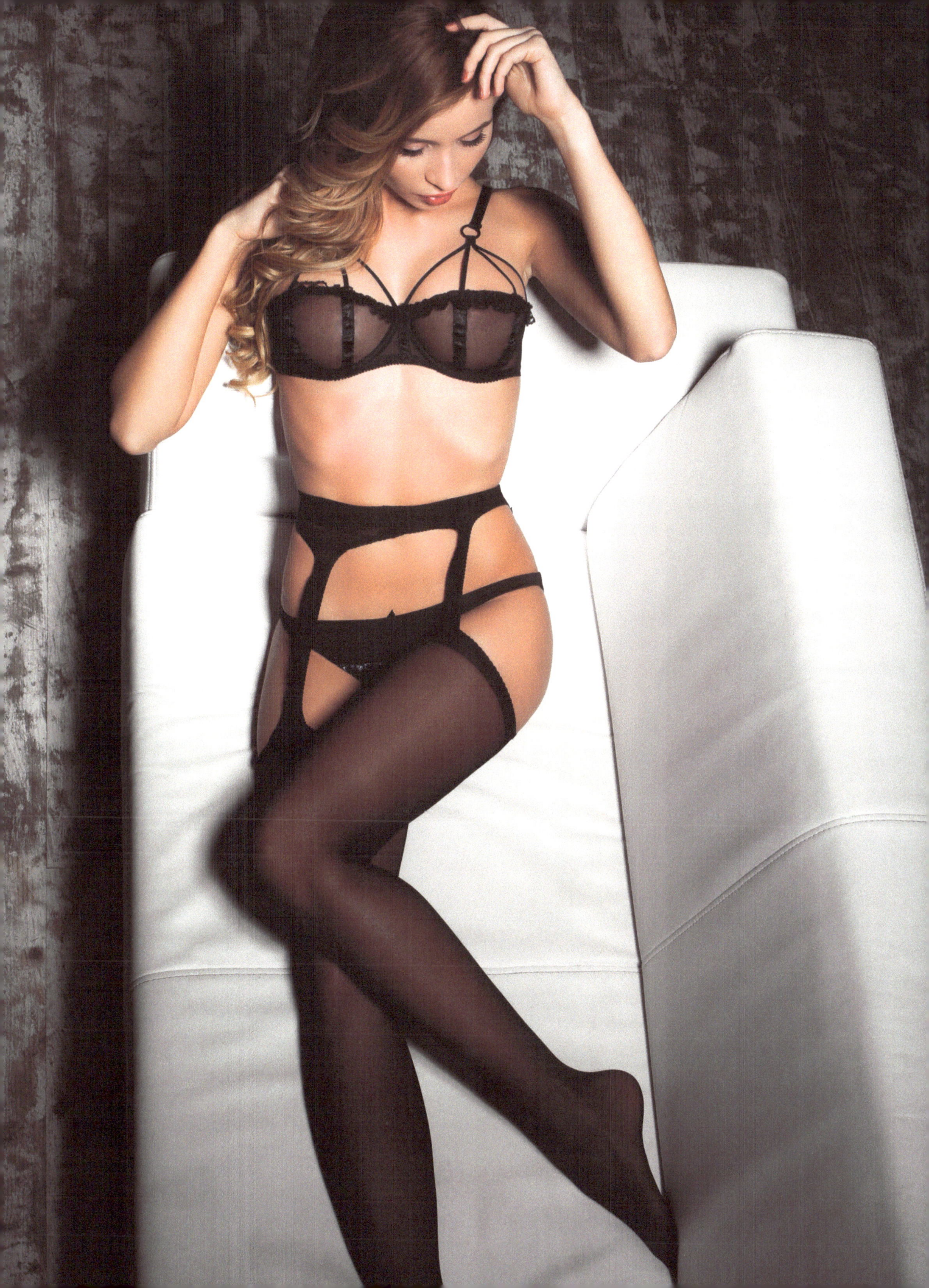

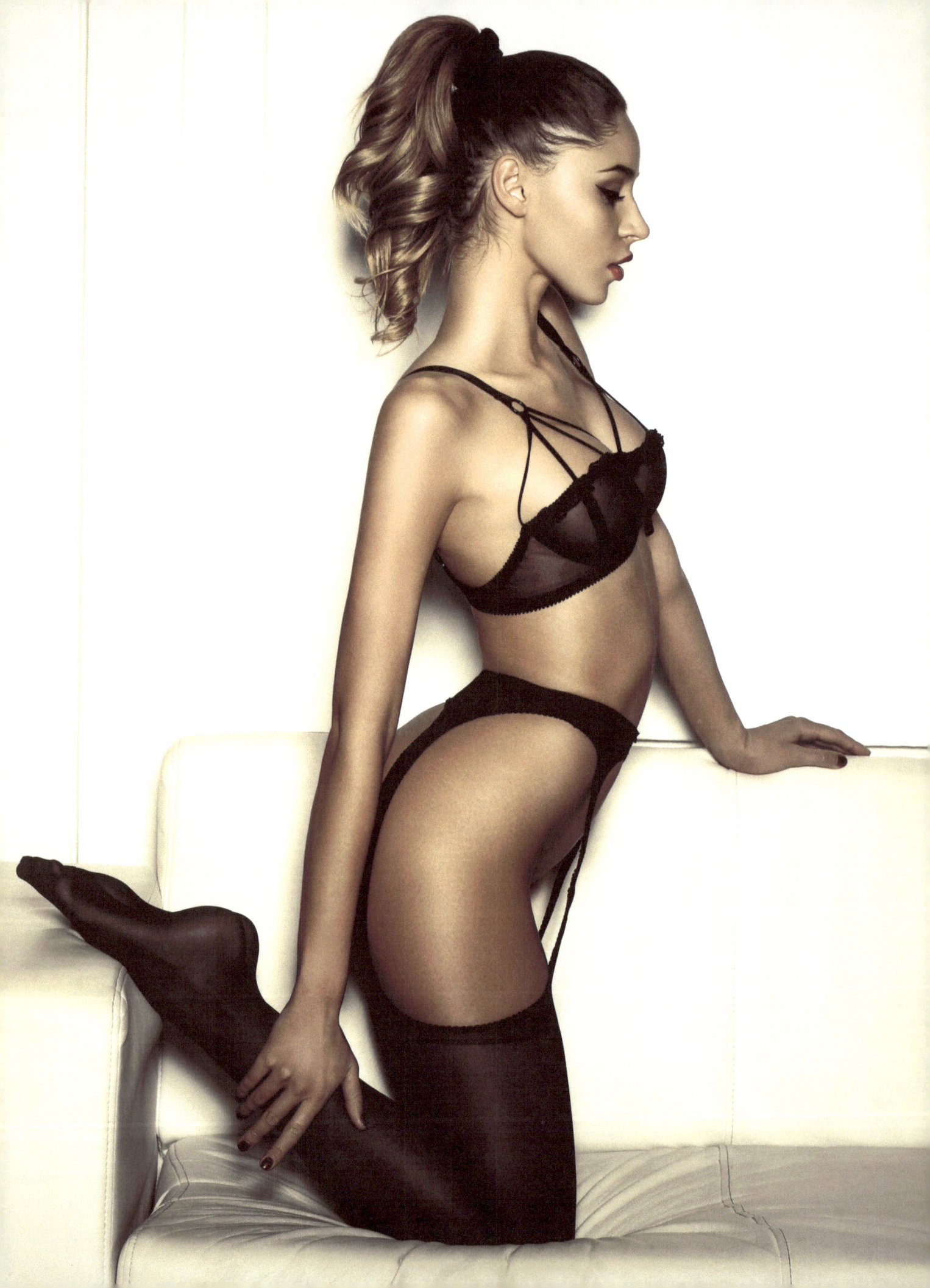

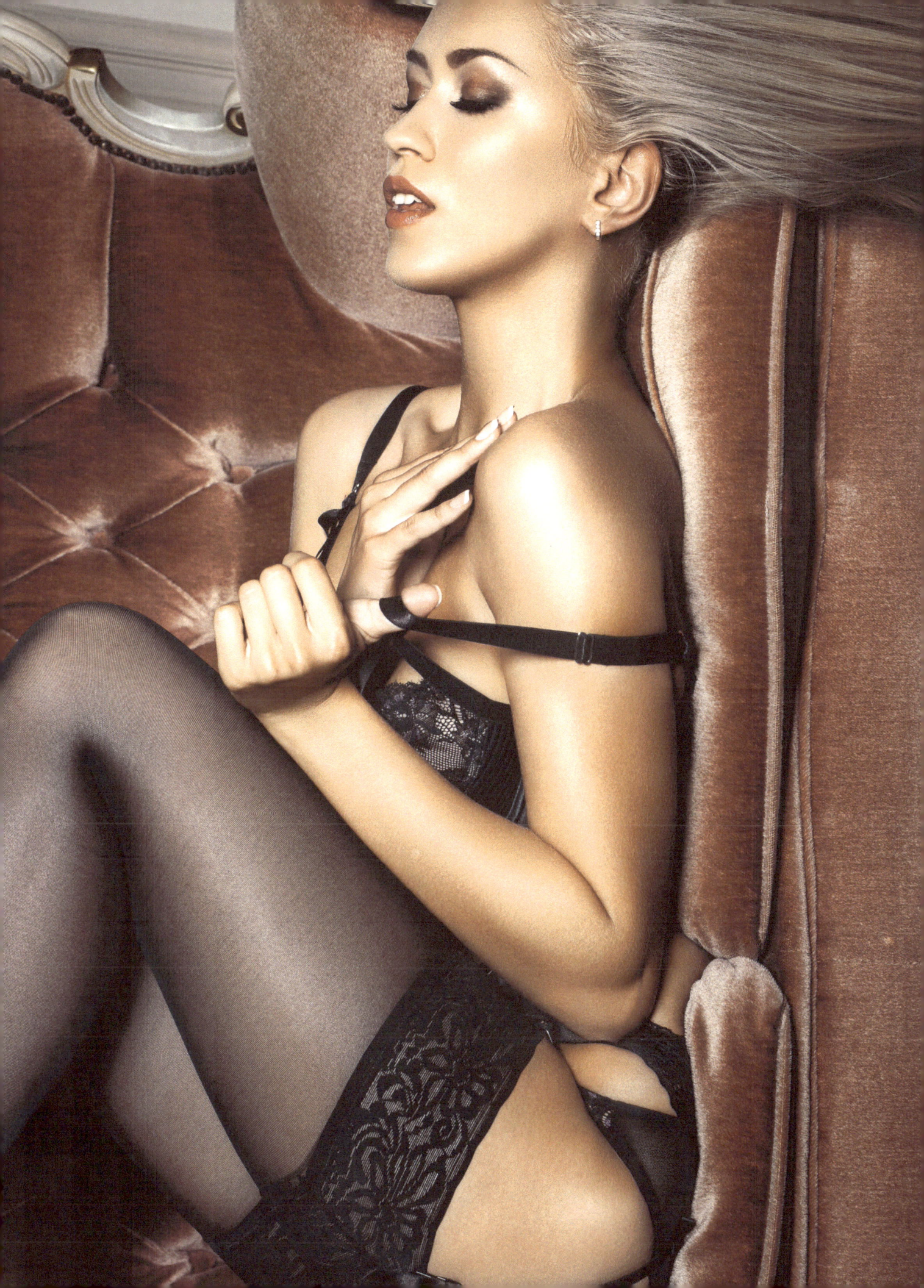

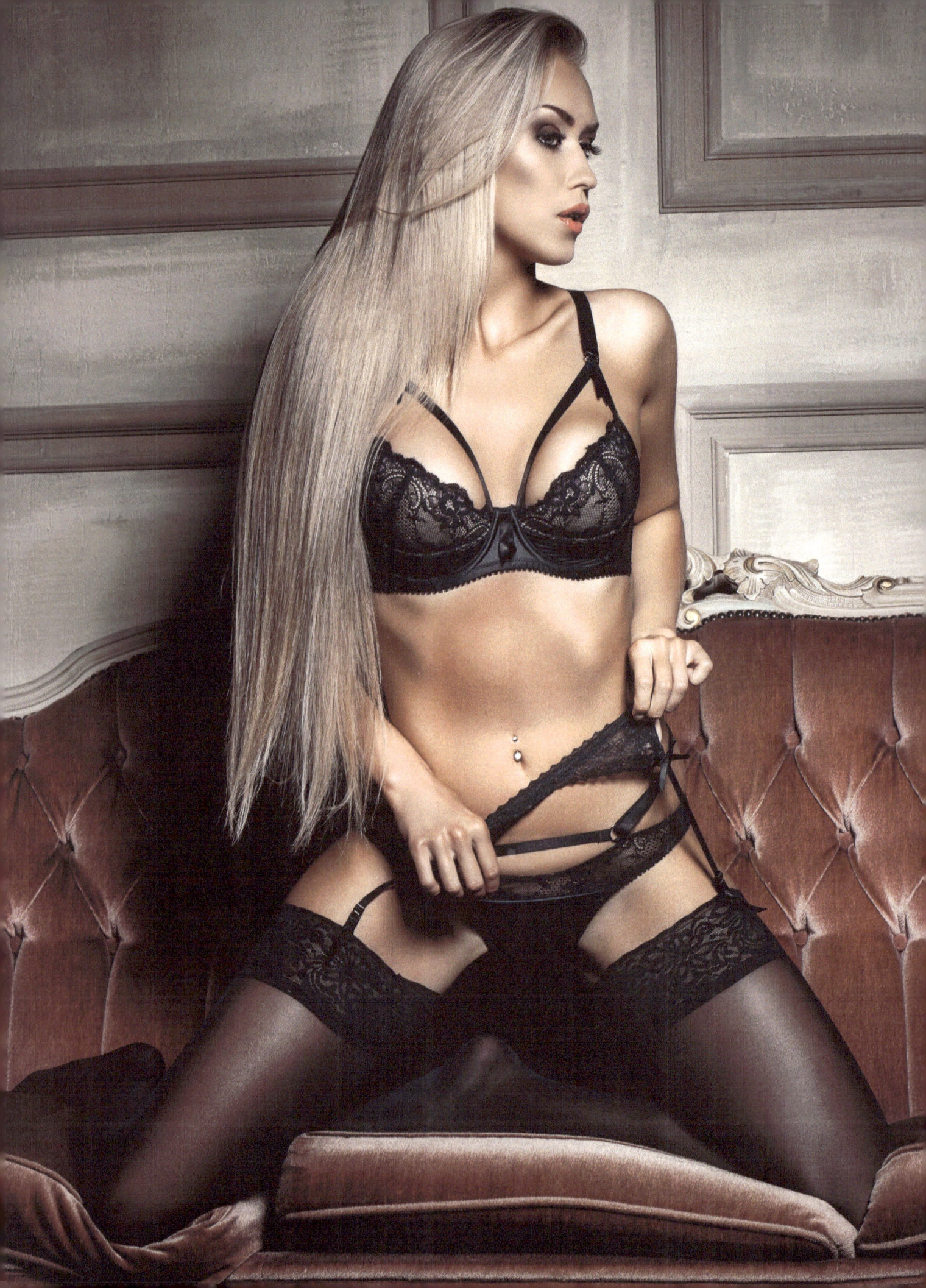

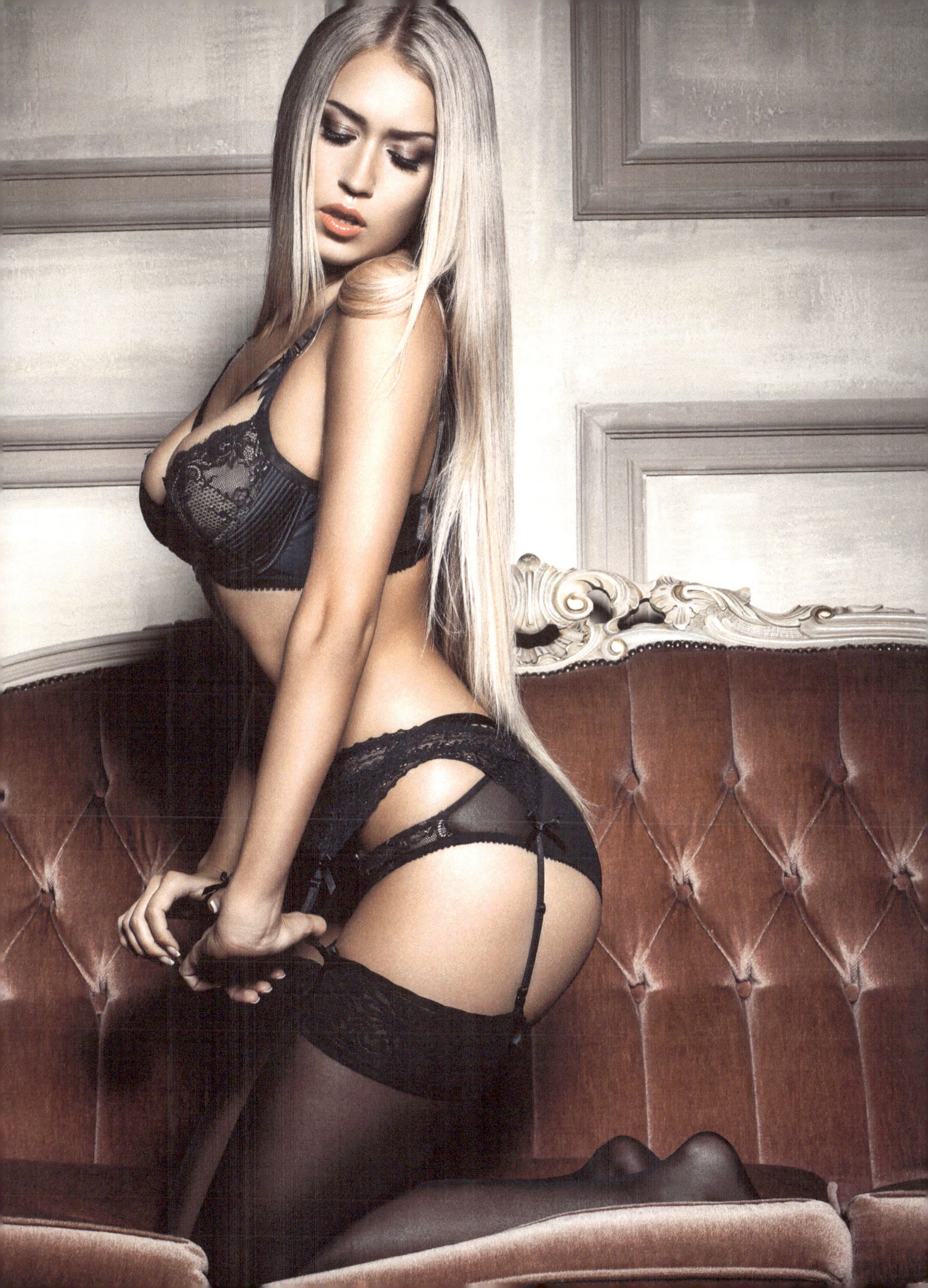

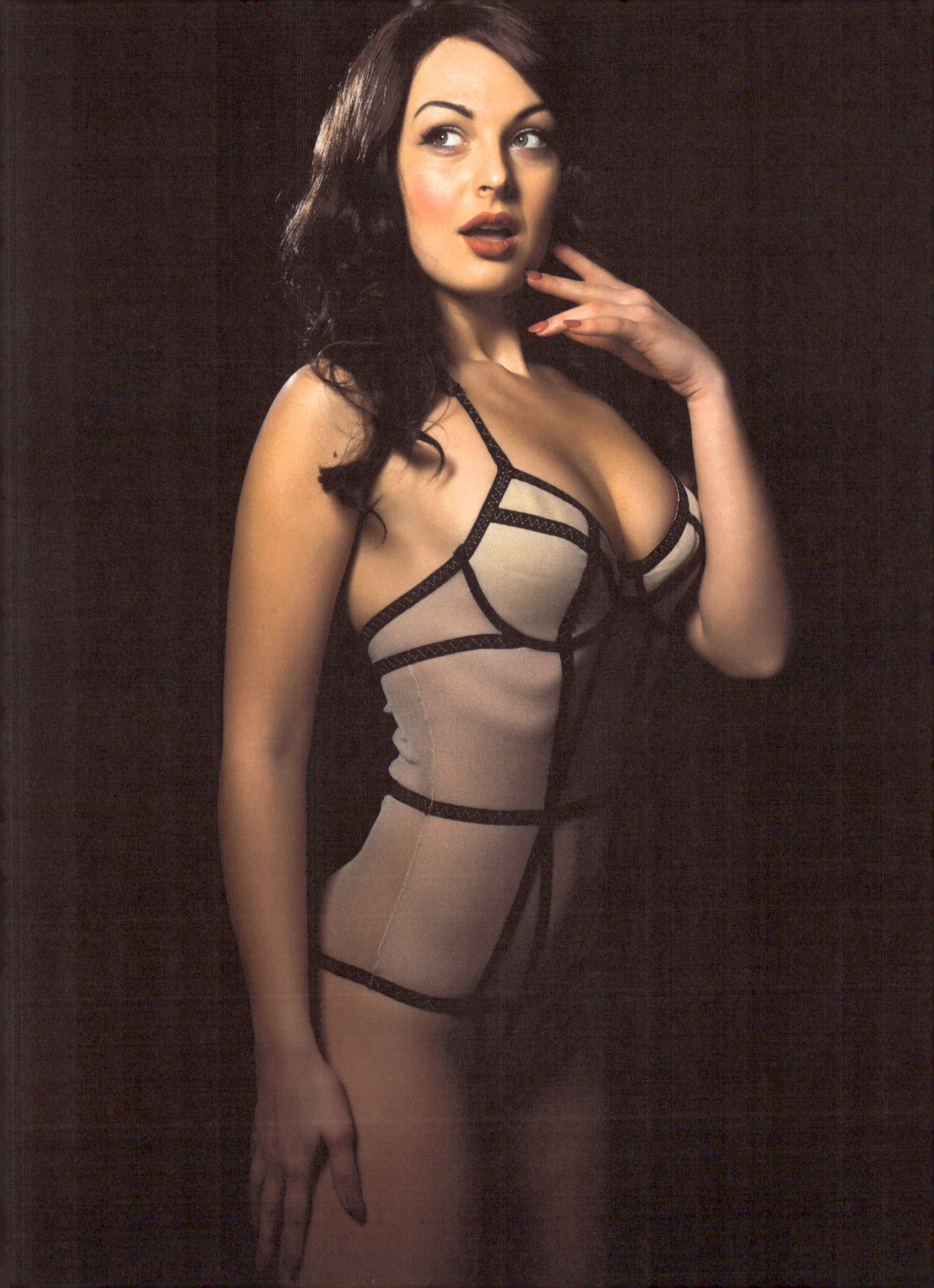

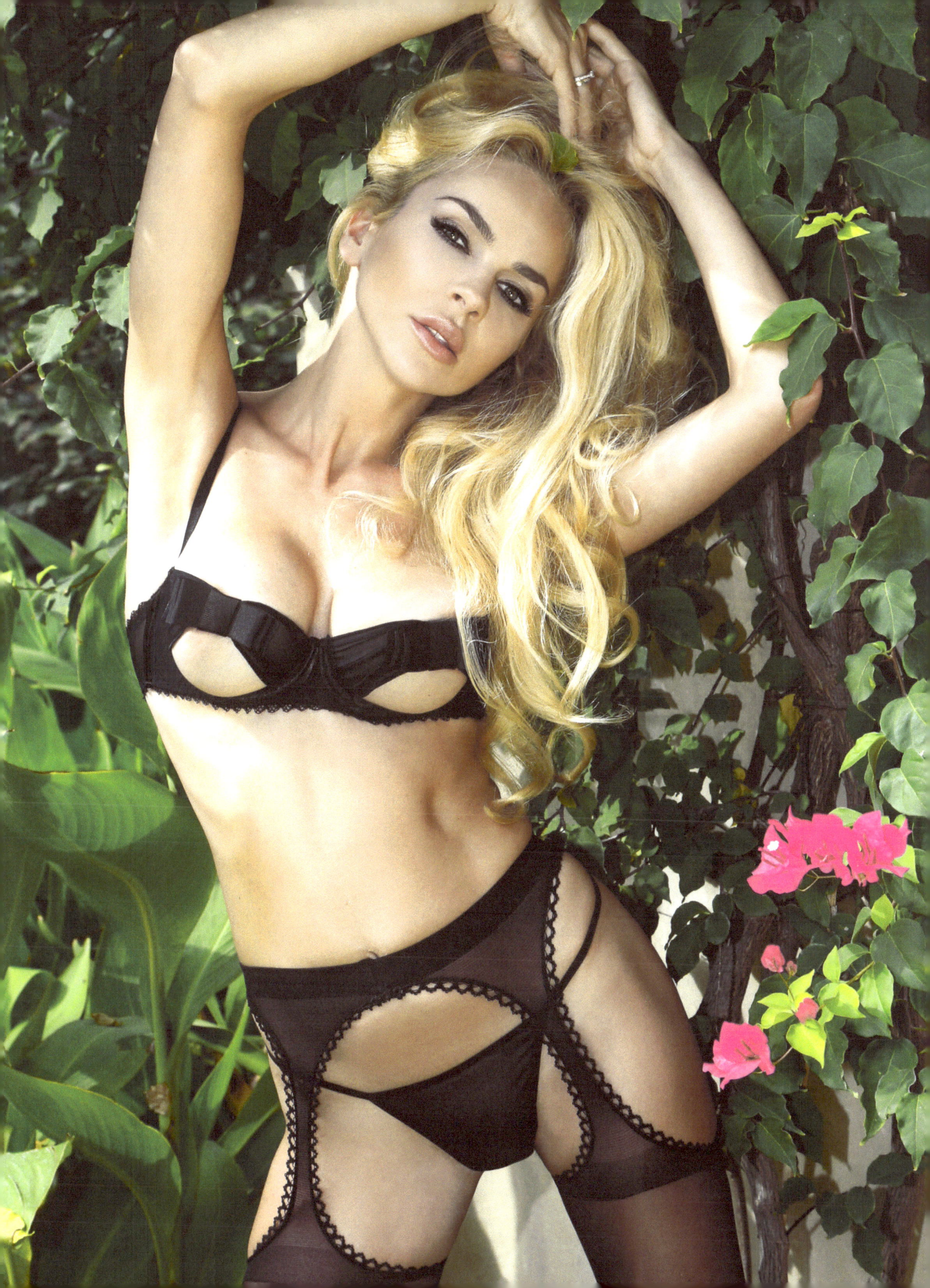

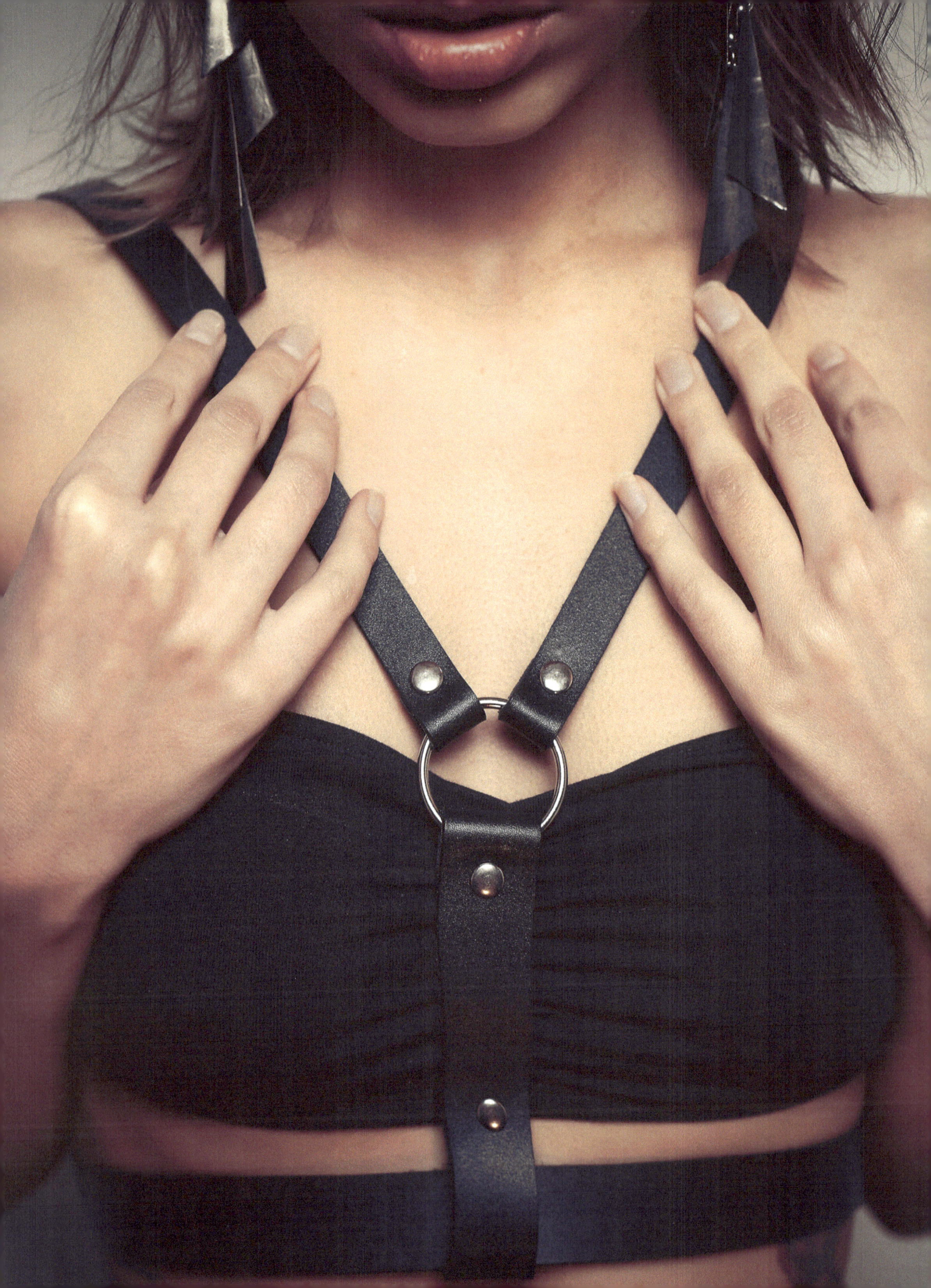

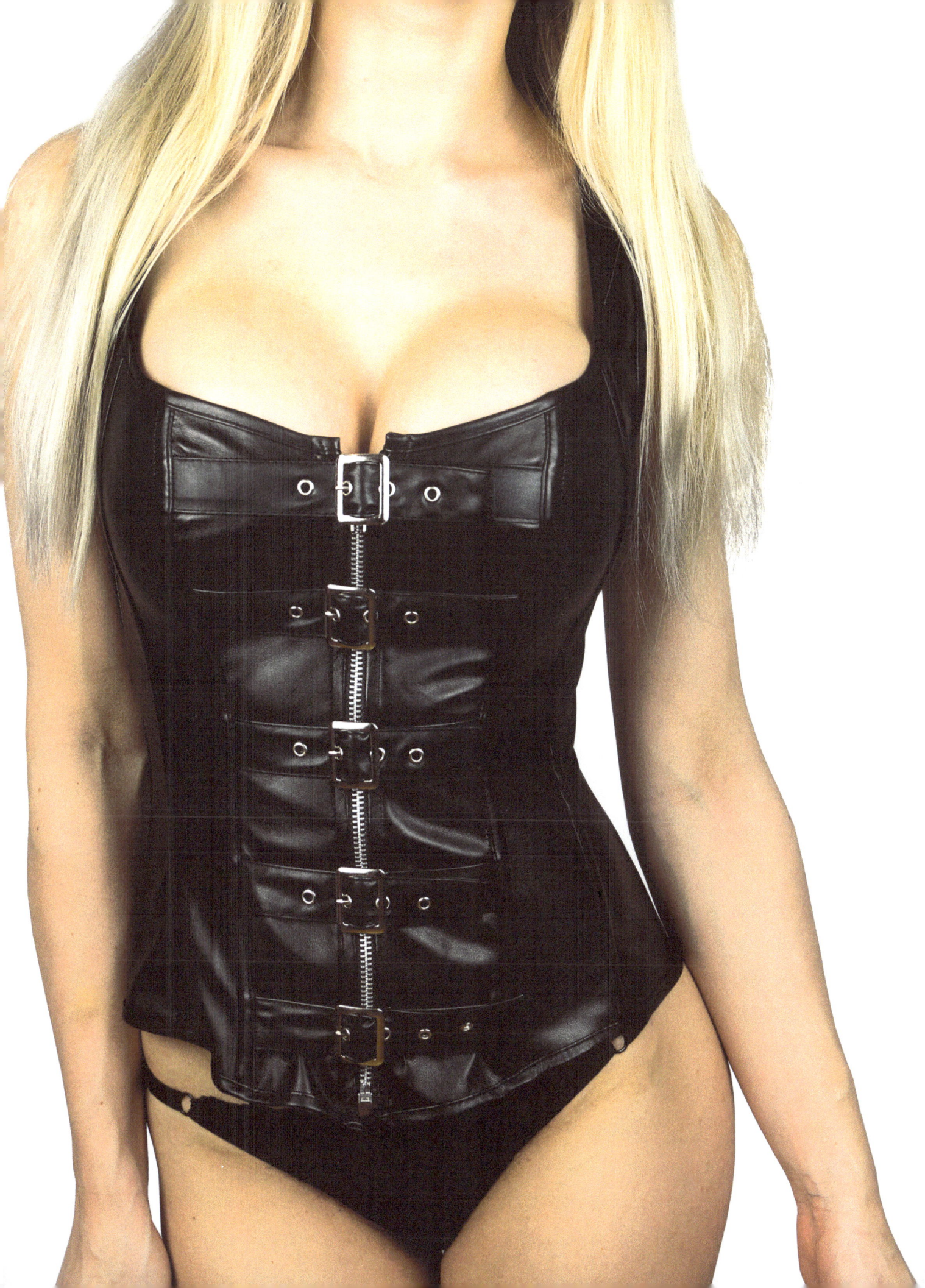

www.ingramcontent.com/pod-product-compliance
Lightning Source LLC
Chambersburg PA
CBHW050422180526
45159CB00005B/2374